Mohamed Khadra is a of Sydney, Australia. He as a leader in education and medicine, internationally and in Australia. He has a degree in Medicine, a PhD and a fellowship of the Royal Australasian College of Surgeons. He also has a postgraduate degree in Computing and a Masters of Education.

His roles have included Inaugural Chair of Surgery at the Australian National University, Pro-vice Chancellor for Health, Design and Science at the University of Canberra, Professor of Surgery and Head of the School of Rural Health for the University of New South Wales. He has won several research prizes, including the Noel Newton Prize for surgical research and the Alban Gee Prize in Urology.

Mohamed is co-founder of the Institute of Technology Australia, an accredited higher-education provider that contributes to social justice by delivering accessible and affordable degrees to students in developing countries. He is also the author of *The Patient: One Man's Journey Through the Australian Healthcare System*.

Praise for *Making the Cut*

'Totally absorbing and brilliantly written . . . Khadra offers a unique and often moving insight into the world of the surgeon' *The Age*

'Unputdownable . . . I read the book straight through one night . . . A tough-minded book, but also full of love . . . Compelling and memorable' *Australian Literary Review*

'Khadra's vignettes are those that so many in our profession of medicine will readily identify with . . . A book well worth reading' *Australian Medicine*

'Gripping' *Sun Herald*

'A very good writer capable of describing the challenges of modern surgery and the modern hospital system . . . provides human insights into people who save lives with a scalpel and rarely a kind word' *Sydney Morning Herald*

'At a time when the health industry faces fresh challenges, this book makes an important contribution to considerations about policies and practices. It deserves to be read widely, especially by health professionals' *Hobart Mercury Magazine*

'I can't wait for him to write another page turner as gripping as this one' *Australian Country Style*

'A fascinating read' *Australian Doctor*

DR MOHAMED KHADRA

A Surgeon's Stories of Life on the Edge

MAKING
THE
CUT

WILLIAM HEINEMANN: AUSTRALIA

A William Heinemann book
Published by Random House Australia Pty Ltd
Level 3, 100 Pacific Highway, North Sydney NSW 2060
www.randomhouse.com.au

First published by Random House Australia in 2007
This edition published by William Heinemann in 2009

Addresses for companies within the Random House Group can be found at
www.randomhouse.com.au/offices.

National Library of Australia
Cataloguing-in-Publication Entry

Khadra, Mohamed.
Making the cut: a surgeon's stories of life on the edge.

ISBN 978 174166 844 5 (pbk.).

Khadra, Mohamed.
Surgeons – Australia – Biography.

617.092

Cover design by Henry Steadman
Internal design by Midland Typesetters, Australia
Typeset in Janson Text by Midland Typesetters, Australia
Printed and bound by Griffin Press

Random House Australia uses papers that are natural, renewable and
recyclable products and made from wood grown in sustainable forests.
The logging and manufacturing processes are expected to conform to
the environmental regulations of the country of origin.

Contents

Acknowledgements   xi
Author's Note   xiii

Part One: Training

1 The First Cut   3
2 Mrs Jones   17
3 At Mortality's Edge   29
4 The Power to Hurt   39
5 To Sleep   53
6 Lucy   67
7 A Punitive God   77
8 The Avoidance Game   89
9 Stabat Mater   97
10 Justice Connolly   107
11 Working Holiday   115
12 A Successful Clone   125

Part Two: Practice

13 Ode on Solitude   135
14 Into the Sunset   149
15 Shem   157
16 Mrs Tobias   167
17 Opiated   175
18 To My Wife   185
19 Julia   197

20 My Mother   205
21 The Sick Rose   217
22 Father Santino   227
23 Ulysses   237
24 O Captain! My Captain!   251
25 Malpractice   261
26 Passing the Torch   271

To MM, who continues to make me the best man I can be, and to BMcC, who made me the best surgeon I could be.

Acknowledgements

I met Shawn Ingham by chance, and after talking with him about his career as a writer, I told him that I had previously written a short story. He wanted to read it. He felt from the start that a larger work about my life as a surgeon needed to be written. From there, our friendship grew with the help of a large number of cappuccinos. He had faith in me and has guided and supported all aspects of this book. He has critiqued, edited, contributed, shaped and assisted the entire process. He is a true mensch.

Sophie Hamley from Cameron Creswell concluded that she was going to support my book having only read the first few pages. Her enthusiasm and utter professionalism as an agent and a friend has been the driving force and the reason this book has found a home at Random House Australia.

No author could have a more supportive and caring publisher than Tim Whiting from Random House. Tim has thoroughly and carefully reviewed the many versions and then involved senior editor Catherine Hill, whose insights and guidance have been invaluable. The team at Random House have been superlative in their professionalism and support for this book.

Of course, I would not be a surgeon without the surgeons who taught me and the residents and nurses with whom I worked.

I would also like to pay tribute to my students, whose poetry sections are such an integral part of this book, and to my patients, who not only instructed me, but taught me about humanity and about life. Every one of them has been a Sufi master in some way.

Also, to my mother (may she rest in peace) and father, without whose sacrifices and support I would never have made it.

Finally, to my wife and boys, who have listened to endless recitals of various passages and who have each contributed to all aspects of this book.

To all, my eternal gratitude.

Author's Note

When I was a Professor of Surgery, I used to conduct surgical tutorials with students. At the end of each tutorial I insisted that students presented a favourite poem that they then recited to the class. At first, they would always fail to see the relevance of poetry with regards to surgery. After a while, they understood that poetry is the study of humanity and we, as surgeons, are intimately and inextricably involved in the study of humanity. How could we hope to perform our task of healing without knowing about humankind, whose characteristics, in distillation, are the very essence of poetry? We attempted in each tutorial to understand this through the voice of masters, in the hope that it may assist us to better work our art as surgeons – that we may alleviate suffering. After each poem, we drew analogies from the poem to stories of patients and how illness brings changes to the very heart of a human who is facing their mortality, their fears and their pain.

This book is an extension of those tutorials. Each chapter starts with a poem and then relates stories about patients, our health system and our professionals. Each of the stories is meant to provoke discussion about health issues I believe society needs to address or to better understand. These stories are presented in the context of my life as a surgeon, from the beginning of my training to my departure.

The book is no more a biography or a faithful historical account of my life as a surgeon than Monet's paintings of Giverny are engineering drawings of a Japanese bridge. If one were pressed for categorisation, impressionistic memoir would come close, but still fail to encapsulate the essence or true intent of this work.

As it stands, the book is a collection of impressions and retellings that are meant to raise issues about health, surgery, death and dying. Yes, my life and my memories are woven into these stories, but in order to enhance the necessary confidentiality of the patients, doctors and hospitals, I have built amalgams of characters and events and fictionalised places and names. In finding names for the characters, I have tried to avoid similarities with anyone I have known or know of. Some of the patients described were not my patients. I have adopted them because their story is powerful and must be told. Yet all the stories here have occurred in one form or another. They are occurring every day in our health systems.

The book is set in the Victoria Hospital. There is no such place as the Victoria Hospital. It, too, is an amalgam of the various hospitals where I trained and later became a consultant and Professor of Surgery.

Within each story, I have tried to imagine for the characters a persona and a life outside my contact with them so as to accentuate their humanity to the reader. I have based these fictional extensions to the patient's story on conversations and snippets of insight I gleaned from my interactions with the doctors who cared for the patients, or with my conversations with the patients themselves.

Another way to view the book is as a health system user's manual for both patients and the health professionals that look after them. Through further understanding, we may all be able to better utilise this vast structure to far greater advantage.

Modern hospital health systems are composed of complex, departmentally segmented fiefdoms led by a bureaucracy that often understands little about the clinical care of the individual. As a consequence, the individual needs to take charge. There is sometimes a feeling among patients that their role is not to question medical advice or treatment. The exact opposite is true – the individual needs to question:

'Is this course of action right for me?'

'What are the alternatives?'

'How else can I return to health?'

'Do I want to live well or live long, or can I achieve both?'

'Who in this hospital is coordinating my care? Who has chased up the pathology results and who is interpreting them?'

'Do I really want to receive this care?'

The classic view of the doctor's role, supported by nurses and technicians, is one of coordinating your information and arriving at a strategic view on how to guide you, the patient, back to good health. But it is unfortunately rare now. It has been replaced by a highly compartmentalised health system with sub-specialists for almost every aspect of the body, often with little if any cohesiveness between them.

There is also the view among many health professionals that it is not acceptable to offer 'no' care – that we must always do something. Knowing when not to act is ultimately the most difficult of all decisions. The pressure is always on the health professional to utilise the latest treatment, or the newest experimental measures.

Sometimes the most humane course is to allow nature to deal with its own.

To be a surgeon is to stand, without flinching, in the sea of human suffering and use our entire resource of knowledge, skill and intelligence to battle it. Our lives are like scenes from a horror movie, where scorpions have covered the face of an individual and we attempt to pick them off before they die. Sometimes we do and sometimes we cannot. Each patient brings with them their unique scorpions of pain or suffering. Sometimes, by picking them off, we make the sting worse. This is the worst of all outcomes.

For the most part, we alleviate the suffering. For the most part, we make people better. For the most part, we regard the honour of alleviating humanity's suffering with enormous gravity.

To become a surgeon, one endures a training program that lasts between seven to ten years after medical school. During that time, a trainee's resolve is tested on a daily basis. No amount of monetary reward compensates the loss of youth, the hours of study, the years of endurance. We become surgeons because we are driven through love. A holy love for a tradition that stretches back to the Stone Age, to Hippocrates, Aesclepius, the barber surgeons of the Middle Ages and then to the formation of the colleges. Character, honour, skill and tradition – this is what makes up a surgical life. Yet surgeons are human too. They suffer, they have illness and they fail.

How a surgeon deals with their own suffering determines how well they make the cut.

PART ONE
Training

CHAPTER 1

The First Cut

If you can keep your head when all about you
Are losing theirs and blaming it on you;
If you can trust yourself when all men doubt you,
But make allowance for their doubting too;
If you can wait and not be tired by waiting,
Or, being lied about, don't deal in lies,
Or, being hated, don't give way to hating,
And yet don't look too good, nor talk too wise;
If you can dream – and not make dreams your master;
If you can think – and not make thoughts your aim;
If you can meet with triumph and disaster
And treat those two impostors just the same;
If you can bear to hear the truth you've spoken
Twisted by knaves to make a trap for fools,
Or watch the things you gave your life to broken,
And stoop and build 'em up with worn-out tools;
If you can make one heap of all your winnings
And risk it on one turn of pitch-and-toss,
And lose, and start again at your beginnings
And never breathe a word about your loss;
If you can force your heart and nerve and sinew
To serve your turn long after they are gone,
And so hold on when there is nothing in you
Except the Will which says to them: 'Hold on';
If you can talk with crowds and keep your virtue,
Or walk with kings – nor lose the common touch;
If neither foes nor loving friends can hurt you;
If all men count with you, but none too much;
If you can fill the unforgiving minute
With sixty seconds' worth of distance run –
Yours is the Earth and everything that's in it,
And – which is more – you'll be a Man my son!

'IF' BY RUDYARD KIPLING

'Scalpel.'

I uttered that time-honoured cliché, which is spoken in a hundred different languages in a thousand hospitals each day. I was being given a chance to perform my first operation long before the other interns in my graduating year and most of the residents the year beyond me had even been allowed to assist other surgeons. Every year the most dedicated, ambitious and hardest-working intern was rewarded with the chance to make their first cut.

It was my first year in a hospital. I had graduated from medical school and had declared my love of surgery to the surgical superintendent. When I was a boy growing up in Ghana, my favourite play was to operate on my teddy bears. I would connect them up with wires to my parents' stereo system and pretend to be the surgeon. After cutting into the stuffing and the fabric, I would then sew them up with needle and thread.

As a medical student, I would spend free weekends assisting in the operating theatres, holding a leg for plastering, running to the ward to get notes, watching. I lived for the atmosphere of theatres. To me, there was no greater calling than to heal, and surgery was the greatest way there was to do so. It was the single reason for my wanting to become a surgeon in the first place.

When in doubt, cut it out. Heal with steel. These were the aphorisms I longed to live by. I knew it was a long road. I knew it was a difficult road. Do your internship. Work hard. Make no mistakes. Get onto the basic surgical scheme for two to three years as a resident and then get accepted onto the advanced training scheme as a registrar for the next four years. During that time, do some research, do your primary examinations and then your fellowship examinations. A seven- to ten-year journey. Here it was, beginning with a single cut.

I had worked hard for this honour. My heart beat fast with the anticipation at the thought of operating. I lived for surgery. I was nothing if not a surgeon. I was the first to arrive each morning and the last to leave. I never left my work to be done by another shift of doctors. At the time, I believed that there was nothing on earth that could compare with the feeling of holding a sharp, sterile blade, about to pierce human flesh – the ultimate control that it provided over another being. I was about to have my first taste of blood.

'Hold on for a moment,' said Dr Agnes Perez, general surgeon at Victoria Hospital, holding my gaze through her bifocals, her gloved hand resting softly on mine. 'Where are you planning to cut?'

'I plan to make an elliptical incision, with a one-centimetre margin around the lesion.' I gave the textbook answer.

The patient had had a general anaesthetic and could not – one hoped – hear the tutorial about to take place around the black spot that his wife had discovered on his back just two weeks earlier. I wondered what his reaction would be if he was aware of the total incompetence of the hand that was now poised, holding a scalpel, right above his flesh.

'Sister, could you get him a marking pen so he can show us exactly how he plans this massacre,' said Dr Perez. The sarcasm escaped the attention of no one in the operating theatre. That is why it's called a theatre: it is the entertainment, the inherent drama that is the pulse of this part of the hospital.

Sister Duncan was the scrub nurse. She looked away, grinning, and asked the scout nurse to get a marking pen.

She knew the routine. Dr Perez had picked one intern each year for the last ten years and had taken them through the same operation – the excision of a skin lesion.

We had to wait for the pen to be brought from central stores. All the while there was silence. I felt a drop of sweat roll down the back of my armpit. I was even more nervous from anticipation and the delay.

The pen arrived.

'Put the scalpel down and pick up the pen and draw where you are going to cut,' ordered Dr Perez.

I drew a line around the lesion, purposely making it more generous to show Dr Perez that I was aware that this lesion was likely to be a melanoma and that complete excision was mandatory.

'OK,' she said.

'Scalpel.' I picked up the knife and was once again poised for action. The blade glinted under the bright lights above. I was aware that everyone was watching intently. Another droplet of sweat rolled down the side of my head. I brought the edge down onto skin.

'How are you going to close this wound, Dr Khadra?' she asked, once again piercing me with her intense Latin eyes. Were she not my boss she would actually have been quite attractive.

I was sure she saw the impatient frustration in my eyes now. She knew that she was prick-teasing. Surgery is better than sex for most surgeons, and being interrupted prior to the ultimate pleasure of incising skin was frustrating. The samurai code, the Bushido, tells us that if a samurai draws their sword, then they must draw blood. A surgeon does not pick up a scalpel to make an opening in skin without having planned the closure. I was a novice and I was now about to be shown how much of novice I was. My excitement and anticipation gave way to dismay.

'I plan to use nylon interrupted sutures.' As soon as I had said this I realised my own stupidity; there was no way that the edges of the wound I had just drawn in ink on this man's back could come together without enormous tension. Tension in a wound would lead to inevitable breakdown and ulceration. I had fallen for the trap. Nurse Duncan tittered. Dr Perez had achieved her objective.

'Golden rule, *hombre*. Think before you cut,' said Dr Perez as she took the pen and traced out a different incision, one that would allow a flap of skin to be developed, which in turn would allow closure without tension.

'OK?' She nodded in the direction of the scalpel once again. This time it was passed to her. She took it. My heart sank. She looked up at me and hesitated for a moment, then passed the scalpel back to me. I took it quickly.

Was there anything else? *Think, you idiot, think.* My mind was blank. I once again hovered over uncut skin, over the lines that she had drawn. I looked at her, hesitating. There was no reaction from her. No clue.

I was about to make my first cut. I could hear nothing but the thumping of my heart, the ventilator and the Bach 'Double Violin Concerto' from the small tape player in the corner. She always had Bach playing when she operated. I slowly brought the knife down onto skin. Her voice suddenly rasped in my ears.

'Do you think you should ask for antibiotics?'

I kept the knife in my hand this time.

'I do not think that there is a need for prophylaxis. The back is relatively clean and this is not a soiled wound,' I replied, giving another textbook answer.

'I always give antibiotics to these patients. I know what the books say, but it's bullshit.' She spoke with measured tones as if to say, 'You should know my standing orders before you presume to work with me, you moron.' She continued, 'I have seen enough of them get infections.'

I turned to the anaesthetist.

'Doctor Margan, would you mind giving one gram of . . .' I looked back at the ogre. 'Are you happy with Keflin, Doctor Perez?'

'I gave a gram of Keflin half an hour ago, Doctor. You should have paid attention,' said Dr Margan, enjoying taking part in the crucifixion.

Clearly there was great pleasure to be had from my utter humiliation. I was now shaking even more than before. Everyone knew it. They all could see the moisture forming two vast semicircles from my armpits; they could see the embarrassed reddening of my face. All could feel the nervous oscillations of the knife in my hand.

'OK,' said Dr Perez, looking at me. 'Go ahead.'

I brought the knife down to the patient's skin and pulled the belly of the scalpel along the lines she had drawn. There was no bleeding. I couldn't understand why not. I looked again and realised that I had hardly scratched the surface of the skin.

'Do you think we could make a hole this time?' Dr Perez said flatly.

There were peals of laughter around the theatre. I tried again, this time going all the way through the dermis, through fat and almost to the muscular layer. The bleeding started. I took the diathermy and got to work excising the lesion and the underlying fat. The bleeding was quite profuse. But I did not stop. It got worse. I looked down at the small puddle of blood forming around my theatre boots. It was the patient's blood seeping through the cloth covers that were a mandatory part of theatre dress and then soaking my socks through the holes in my shoes. My anxiety coupled with my inexperience had won the day.

'Is this patient cross-matched, Doctor Margan?' Dr Perez was looking at me as she asked the question.

This was her ultimate insult. To ask about a blood cross-match for excision of a skin lesion is a sarcastic way to say, 'Do you think you should do something about the blood loss?' More titters from her audience. I handed her the diathermy, which is used to cauterise bleeding vessels. She took it and along with a pair of forceps stopped one arterial bleeder, which was now flooding my operative site and the drapes. I found it hard to believe that all this came from one artery. I should have looked closer. I should have controlled my anxiety better.

A sponge deftly mopped the remaining blood and I could once again see the edges of the wound. Dr Perez handed back the diathermy. The movement said, 'You have a lot to learn, little man.'

I miraculously kept going till the end. When it came to closing the wound, each stitch had to be redone because it was too shallow or too deep, too near the edge of the wound or too far away. When the dressings finally went on I had no sense of triumph, no pride about what I had done. I felt utter humiliation. I had hatred in my belly for every member of that theatre. Did they know it? Did they care?

'I'll see you back on the ward,' said Dr Perez, as she left the theatre.

I wrote up the notes, got the post-op orders organised, changed out of the theatre gown and ran to the ward, but she had already gone. She had left some orders about one or two patients.

Later, when I got to the cafeteria, there were derisory glances from several of my colleagues. I chose to sit by myself. My registrar, John Redman, came over. He was in his eighth year of training and was about to graduate as a consultant, an attending medical practitioner – a fully trained surgeon.

'I heard about what happened. We've all been through it, mate. You did well.' He needed to say that in order to ensure that I wouldn't take myself out that very day. There had been a spate of junior doctor suicides and another one would certainly not look good for the great and ancient Victoria Hospital. As my registrar, he had a duty of care. He had been an intern. He had gone through the nightmare years of residency and had survived the advanced training scheme for surgery – a difficult and selective pathway open to few. The term registrar was the differentiator, allowing one to be known as a trainee surgeon. Some say the registrar years are the happiest in surgery.

'I'm okay, John,' I said, smiling broadly. Any emotion now and you were regarded as a soft touch. It only needed a whisper for your career to be over – 'He is a bit of a wimp' or 'I worry whether he can stick it out'. I was not going to give them the satisfaction of seeing the pain of my humiliation. *Fuck you. Fuck you all*, I thought.

What was supposed to have been a triumph had turned into a disaster. What was a reward had become a punishment. Fundamentally, these harrowing events in our training, of which there were many, did one of two things. They destroyed the trainee, no matter what stage of their training they were at, or they built character, the type of character that a surgeon needs to make life and death decisions without flinching or faltering. Surgical training was seen as a baptism by fire. What does not kill you makes you stronger.

For centuries, surgeons had been taught by fear and humiliation. The assumption was that you needed to learn by having your fear centres stimulated. Humiliation taught you to respect the adverse outcomes that are possible despite the best intentions and efforts, the unexpected deaths, the complication that you are blamed for where negligence played no part. The humiliation taught you about life's unexpected end, and it was meant to give the trainee the realisation that every operation could very well end in disaster. The sooner you learned this lesson, the sooner you could progress as a competent surgeon.

This process of training was a Darwinian method to ensure that only those who could cope with the pressure of surgery survived. There is nothing on Earth worse than a weak, indecisive surgeon, and lying in wait to weed out the weak and the undesirable were five years of medical school, three years of basic training, then four years on the surgical training scheme – more on-the-job fear and humiliation than most humans will ever have to endure.

You cannot learn until you accept your own ignorance. I came out of medical school with an arrogance about my position and title as a 'doctor', having passed final year at the top of the heap, as I had in the final year of high school and in the final year of primary school. As an intern, I now found myself at the bottom of a very large heap.

Dr Perez was fond of telling a story about an interview for a new surgical trainee that she had participated in. While preparing for the next candidate, the panel was chatting about the number of unintentionally adverse outcomes they had had with a very simple procedure they all performed each day. The next candidate came into the room to be interviewed. He had a good curriculum vitae and had spent his mandatory four years of basic training with numerous glowing reports. One of the surgeons on the panel asked him whether he had performed the particular type of operation they had just been discussing.

He answered, 'Oh yes. I have performed six of them.'

The panel, each member having performed hundreds and respecting the implicit difficulty of the operation, nodded in mock admiration.

'How did you find them?' one of panel then asked.

'A cinch!' was the reply.

Unanimously, the panel decided that the candidate needed another year on the basic training roster as a resident before being admitted to more advanced surgical training in order to gain respect for the operations he performed and the potential for disaster inherent to each.

Surgery is one of the last bastions of the apprenticeship educational model. Medical educationalists have been attempting to change the surgical apprenticeship to competency-based training, attempting to eradicate the centuries-old edict of 'See one, do one, teach one'. This is of course simplifying a very complex process. The idea of a surgical apprenticeship is to assist in an operation, observing carefully what the surgeon (the master) is doing. Then you attempt to do the operation with the surgeon supervising you, and, finally, you are expected to master the operation to the extent of being able to teach it to others. Competency training dictates that there are certain skill levels to be achieved. You are supervised and coached until you achieve the skill levels. Not as exciting perhaps, but a safer method of training than the apprenticeship.

*

Single surgical trainees seemed to survive the ordeal better than the married ones. 'Knife before wife before life' – that was the motto, the code by which those of us who undertook to become surgeons lived by. The knife was surgery and patient care. That took precedence over family life, represented by the spouse. That, in turn, took precedence over life – parties, hobbies, anniversaries, birthdays, and all else that was self-related.

There were 120-hour weeks and on-call shifts that lasted 72 hours with no sleep. There were countless special occasions that you could not attend; fights with your loved ones who felt you were working too hard. At best, you had a 50 per cent chance of attending your son's speech night, birthday or your own wedding anniversary. Often you came home to the cold silence of an unhappy spouse.

I was married during my medical-school days. However, my wife was on her own specialty-training scheme and so she understood all too well. The fact that we were married was irrelevant to the hospital. To them, we were simply two residents and then, later, registrars on their respective training schemes.

Outside the theatres, a surgeon is unreliable. They will not remember to pick up the milk or the dry-cleaning, they will not remember that today is the day they promised to pick up the kids from school and they will fall asleep in the opera. If you marry a surgeon, then expect these things as the norms of life.

There are countless things on the mind of every surgeon. There are the life-and-death decisions you have to make on the spot, day in and day out. The worry that the surgery you perform today is going to fall apart. There is the nagging feeling that the advice given to a patient may have been wrong. There is the firing of junior staff. There is no room here for being a wimp or a sap.

Stories of surgical disasters are the most riveting conversations we have as surgeons.

'Did you hear about John Smith . . . he took out the wrong kidney!'

'I was in theatre with Jacob Major today . . . he could not get out a simple appendix . . . it took him three hours. You should have seen the bleeding.'

These disaster stories helped us realise that even though we were doctors, each one of us is human – that others, too, make mistakes – and that the icy mask that some of our colleagues wore belied a vulnerable and imperfect human.

*

It was not easy during my first year of surgical training. Protestations by my bosses that it was so much harder in their day did not take away the sting of humiliations, the pain of belittlement and the relentless siege of soul that becoming a surgeon entailed.

Yet pain is suppressed or quickly forgotten by humans and so I did not doubt that, in years to come, I would look back on my training and think only of the happy times. I had seen it among women in childbirth, aching and writhing with unfathomable pain written on their faces, who return a year or two later to have another child. The ability to live beyond pain is probably one of the reasons why the human species has survived.

Years later, after I had become a Professor of Surgery, I would walk through the operating theatre, going in to observe tutorials and teaching first-hand. Dr Perez always treated me with respect – she had to. As soon as I left the room, she would no doubt turn to her assistant and tell them about my first operation.

CHAPTER 2

Mrs Jones

When I am an old woman I shall wear purple
With a red hat that doesn't go and doesn't suit me.
And I shall spend my pension on brandy and summer gloves
And satin sandals and say we've no money for butter.
I shall sit down on the pavement when I'm tired
And gobble up samples in shops and press alarm bells
And run my stick along the public railings
And make up for the sobriety of my youth.
I shall go out in my slippers in the rain
And pick flowers in other people's gardens
And learn to spit
You can wear terrible shirts and grow more fat
And eat three pounds of sausages at a go
Or only eat bread and pickle for a week
And hoard pens and pencils and beermats and things in boxes.
But now we must have clothes that keep us dry
And pay our rent and not swear in the street
And set a good example for the children.
We must have friends to dinner and read the papers
But maybe I ought to practise a little now?
So people who know me are not too shocked and surprised
When suddenly I am old and start to wear purple.

'WARNING' BY JENNY JOSEPH

Mrs Jones was a defiant, headstrong woman. She had survived two world wars, six prolonged deliveries, the Depression and the deaths of her husband and two of her children. She smoked. She drank. She ate great big creamy iced buns – despite being a diabetic – that sent her sugar levels off the Richter scale. All who knew her loved her.

My challenge, as the most junior member of the surgical team, was to ensure that our surgical beds were not clogged up with medical patients. Initially, Mrs Jones had been admitted for a deep venous thrombosis of the left calf and was on Heparin to thin her blood. Despite this being a simple medical illness that should have been cared for by the physicians and had Mrs Jones assigned to a medical bed, she had been wrongly admitted under the surgical team. Her thrombosis was assumed to be a post-operative complication. It was not.

In Mrs Jones's case, I had failed by allowing her to take up one of our valuable surgical beds, hence reducing the number of surgical patients we could admit. Dr Perez was not pleased.

The next morning I paid Mrs Jones a visit about a urinary tract infection. I could smell it as soon as I entered the ward – *pseudomonas aeruginosa* has a very distinctive odour. The ancients used their five senses to diagnose disease; we used the pathology lab. Despite the unmistakably specific odour and the high cost of confirming the obvious, I knew I would have to send urine off to the lab so that they could let me know, officially, that this was indeed a urinary tract infection with *pseudomonas*. This was a small issue, however. The fact that her heart had stopped was more important.

I was alerted to this turn of events in the hospital cafeteria, having not eaten for over 24 hours. I had just settled down to a hearty, unrecognisable soup and another stale bread roll in an endless stream of stale bread rolls when my beeper sounded that shrill, impossible-to-ignore page signalling a cardiac arrest. I held it to my ear while looking down at the full tray of uneaten food I had just placed on the table. '*Cardiac arrest. Ward 7, bed 4 . . . Cardiac arrest. Ward 7, bed 4.*' I recognised the patient instantly: Mrs Jones.

I had been on call for 36 hours and still had another 24 hours to go. Being on call for long hours was a hallmark of my training to come, but as an intern on the surgical team, no one in the hospital worked harder. Internship was the first year post medical school. The doctor was expected to do a number of different rotations, each ten weeks long, to experience the breadth of medicine so that they could decide in which specialty they wished to undertake basic training for the following three years of their residency. It was hard to get an internship at the Victoria Hospital. It was a top-tier hospital and was my first choice. I was so glad to have been selected to do my internship here and I had manoeuvred myself into as many surgical terms as was legally possible. As a consequence, I spent the year almost constantly on call.

The Victoria Hospital had been built during the Second World War as a temporary hospital for the overflow of injured soldiers from the Pacific. Fifty years later it was still functioning and, in fact, had been expanded with the addition of a large multistorey building complex that housed several wards, offices, radiology and pathology services.

The remainder of the wards were spread out over a five-acre property. Some wards were so far away that it would take up to twenty minutes of fast walking to get to them. Cardiac arrests in these wards usually meant cardiac deaths, as there was no way for the team to get there in time to resuscitate patients in that golden three-minute window, which often meant the difference between reversible and irreversible brain ischaemia – an inadequate blood supply to the brain. Ward 7 was one such ward.

I started the run, turning left out of the cafeteria and then moving down the long covered pathways that connected one fibro building to the next. I ran like a lion with a white mane, my coat flapping behind me as I passed patients in wheelchairs, doctors on slow, intense teaching ward rounds, medical students with books under their arms and cleaning staff smoking behind columns. I always had a sense of importance as I ran to these arrests. In the years to come I would dread them, but during those early years I sometimes used to wish for them – they punctuated my day and provided a much-needed diversion.

When I finally reached the ward, all the signs of a cardiac arrest were well and truly present. The curtains around the other patients' beds had been closed so that they were somehow excluded from death. No one wanted the reminder, a reminder that they could be next. The ward was not called 'God's waiting room' for nothing. It had earned that name because generations of souls had been quietly dispatched night after night into the afterlife.

There was Eliza Jones, all 120 kilograms of grandmother. It had already been seven minutes since the time of arrest. There was a nurse doing cardiac massage and a medical registrar was attempting to intubate the patient – this would allow control of her airway. Others arrived within seconds. There were now almost twenty doctors, nurses, orderlies, medical students, administrators and intensive-care-unit (ICU) staff. The 'arrest circus' was about to begin.

The first overwhelming impression of an arrest is the pungent odour of vomitus, usually mixed with faeces and almost always with urine. The combination of these smells invades your olfactory nerve endings and then advances into the sinuses and air pockets throughout the skull, such that small amounts of it are then released continuously throughout the remainder of the day. The same smell is to be found in the morgue. Perhaps it is what the ancients called the 'smell of death'.

In Mrs Jones's case the smell was particularly odious as there was also a gangrenous leg ulcer where skin had been placed some five days prior but had not taken. The liquid seeping from her had soaked into the bed on which she lay.

I took up my usual position, labelling the tubes of blood tests and writing the forms for the pathology lab to analyse the chemical that had brought about the release of Mrs Jones into the afterlife. Everyone in the room knew that she was a dead woman. But everyone continued to play the 'arrest circus' game.

No one played the game and taunted the Angel of Death more heroically and deftly than medical registrar Dr Harrison. He had cheated the Angel out of hundreds of patients in his short career. He now focused his eyes on the ECG being generated in a long strip out of the defibrillator.

It was a nurse who spoke up first. 'She didn't want any of this,' she said, frantic, insistent and completely out of place. 'She wanted to be allowed to die!' There were tears welling in her eyes.

Mrs Jones was a lady who had lived with constant pain from legs that were making a desperate attempt to die before she did. She pleaded daily for death to relieve her from the suffering of a body long past its used-by date. She was a burden on her family, on society, and provided a constant source of heartache for the hundreds of hospital doctors and nurses she had come in contact with during her thirty-five admissions to hospital in the last twelve years.

However, between Mrs Jones lying on the bed, heart silent, and the Angel of Death hovering at the door of the ward – urging her soul to join him – was a vast army of modern medical miracle workers.

'Is she documented?' asked Dr Harrison, ever-pragmatic. He did things by the book; there was no room for flagrant emotionalism in his world.

Being documented meant that there was an order signed by either the patient or the next of kin whereby, in the event of a cardiopulmonary arrest, resuscitation was not indicated. This was a rare ticket out of God's waiting room. The patient whose family had been decent enough to secure this ticket for them got to have a special sticker placed in the front of their notes in big black letters. 'NFR' – Not For Resuscitation. Dr Harrison was not going to let Mrs Jones ride the heaven-bound bus without that ticket.

Informing the family that they can, in discussion with the patient, declare a patient 'NFR' is vital and yet rarely done. How does one help the family to evaluate how best to express love to their loved one in hospital? Many seem to feel that to deny their relative even extreme medical measures, when their life is already full of pain and anguish, might be regarded as callous. However, letting nature take its course is sometimes the only natural and humane way for life to be extinguished before dignity is lost. Love can be expressed through a lack of medical care.

'We have been trying to contact the family,' the nurse answered, struggling to maintain composure.

Meanwhile, *thump, thump, thump* – the cardiac massage. *Crunch, crunch, crunch* – the ribs breaking under the weight.

Dr Harrison, barely containing his disdain for the nurse, turned back to the patient.

'Intracardiac adrenaline!'

Dr Harrison was going to town on this one. His hand reached out for the syringe a nurse had just drawn up with adrenaline. He injected it into the front of the chest, down deep into the heart itself. As he did so he kept his eye on the monitor in front of him. The high priest was consulting the oracle, using this herb, burning that incense.

We all stood in awe at the processes of life as it returned to Mrs Jones. First one beat; then another. Now a blood pressure. Dr Harrison looked around as if staring straight into the Angel's eyes that were now filled with tears of defeat and sadness.

'Yeeeesssssss!'

Medicine, 1. Death, 0.

Here was the might of twenty-first-century Western medicine with its beautifully focused approach to specific diseases pitted against the forces of nature. This game was what it was all about. This fight for life over death was the object of our existence as modern doctors. This is why we had big teaching hospitals, training schemes that the third world envied, technology which – without a second thought or regard to cost – was provided to all who needed it.

Your taxes have paid for this magnificent machine called a health system. These public hospitals were staffed with young trainees whose careers depended on getting you the best outcome. Elongating your life was their challenge.

You may wait for your operation; your room might be dirty; you might end up with a hospital-acquired infection – but someone has to provide the material on which our future doctors train, and you, the Medicare patient, are elected. The biggest of the public hospitals made no pretence and were called teaching hospitals. There is full disclosure before you walk in. You will be involved in the teaching of our next generation of doctors. In fact, your body will be the teacher.

These teaching hospitals also had the latest and best of all technologies and the cost of running them was enormous. Sadly, there is very little wisdom in how the tax dollars are spent. The budgeting process does not allow for wisdom. About 70 per cent of the health budget is spent on caring for patients in their last six months of life. The technologies are not rationed to the cases that most need them. Hence, someone like Mrs Jones might consume a large chunk of the health budget while waiting lists for hip replacements or simple hernias blow out to years.

The urgent need trumps the non-urgent need. That is why private insurance rates are so high. Patients have figured out that they need to go to the private hospitals to get care for the non-urgent, so-called 'elective' operations.

The discussion needs to be had about how society wants to spend its health dollars. Do we want to create criteria that determines whether a patient will be placed on the 'do everything' list or, alternatively, the 'keep comfortable until they die' list? These criteria do exist. There are statistical criteria capable of predicting from the outset (the day of presentation to casualty) the percentage chance that a patient will live or die.

Perhaps someone has to get brave enough to apply these statistical predictors so that health dollars are not wasted.

Of course, this is an economic rationalist's view. It is vastly different when it is applied to an individual and that individual happens to be related to you. Love is such a confounder.

'This is crazy.'

Now where was this new blasphemy coming from, I wondered.

'What are we doing resuscitating this woman?'

It was Joan Gardiner, the social worker. 'What the fuck are we doing here?' she muttered.

She was talking to me. I shrugged my shoulders in a noncommittal way; I was not keen to stick my neck out on this one so early in my career. Did I agree with what was happening? No, but it was not my call. My job was to label the tubes. There were more important things in life than joining Gardiner's futile crusade to protest the needless resuscitation of Mrs Jones. There was an impression I had to create as a member of this elite team of doctors.

I already did not fit in. I was not yet one of the establishment. No one called 'Mohamed' could possibly have been part of that pedigree – I was tainted, in this society, by my Lebanese mother and father's insistence on naming me after the Holy Prophet.

Joan Gardiner looked accusatorily at Dr Harrison. He smiled his disarming smile, triumphant at that moment as any warrior could be. He was Caesar, Alexander the Great and Kublai Khan rolled into one. He had just used his might and power to win the ultimate battle once again – no social worker was going to rain on his parade with moralistic ranting. Certainly not Joan Gardiner, whose lesbian feminist tendencies disgusted him.

Dr Harrison walked away to announce to the family – who had just moments before piled into the waiting area, breathless – his success at resuscitating their loved one. No family ever said, 'You should have let her die, Doctor.' They did not dare. They all mouthed gratitude.

'What will happen now, Doctor?' They wanted to know where they were going to have to spend the next few weeks visiting their grandmother and whether it was close to a car park or not.

'She will be transferred to the intensive care unit and once she is stable she will be sent back to the ward.' The family had old-world values: the doctor was the high priest and they respected him beyond question.

I hung around as the nurses packaged up Mrs Jones's various monitors, drips and the ventilator. The orderly who had been standing outside smoking was called and, together with a nurse, I escorted Mrs Jones up to the intensive care unit. This was the most expensive hotel in the world. A night in ICU could cost the taxpayer as much a night in the presidential suite at the Waldorf-Astoria in New York. For that you got your own nurse every shift and a comfortable bed. Unfortunately, you got no view, no room service and you had to share the room with complete strangers.

A week later, Mrs Jones, still desperate to die, was up in ICU on a ventilator with several drips, heart-sustaining dopamine, a catheter and monitoring.

Dr Joseph Kigali was the new resident for ICU. He turned up for his shift at 4 pm. He had been trained in Nairobi, Kenya, and had obtained a work permit in the Victoria Hospital on a special government visa that encourages doctors trained in the developing nations to come to developed countries to alleviate the perceived shortage of practitioners. For the doctors, it is a ticket to escape a lifetime of near poverty, of working in ill-equipped hospitals, and a chance to give their children an opportunity to study and live in a First World country. Doctors stream out of countries like India, Pakistan and more recently Nigeria, Ghana and Kenya to stock up the corridors of Western hospitals. The shortage of doctors in the West is, of course, relative. In some of the Western countries where these doctors go, the ratio of doctor to the population may be as low as 1:1000 or, in some rural areas, even 1:5000. However, they have left behind countries where the ratios can be 1:100,000.

Dr Kigali was allotted Mrs Jones as one of his patients. He reviewed her notes thoroughly, saw her status and conferred with the nurse looking after Mrs Jones about her condition and care. He noticed that her blood sugar levels were higher than usual.

'I think we had better increase her insulin dose to compensate for this. Are you giving it subcutaneously?' he asked the nurse.

'No, we have an infusion running,' she answered with her back to him.

Dr Kigali looked at the infusion machine. What he would have done for such a machine back at Moi General Hospital in Eldoret, the small rural Kenyan town where he had practiced. He caressed it gently. He had never used one.

'Do you mind dialling up the infusion you want?' The nurse still had her back to him.

He looked at the dials on the front of the machine. He had no clue how to use it, but it shouldn't be that hard to figure out. He certainly was not going to show his ignorance to this female nurse. He pressed several buttons gingerly and then dialled in a new number in order to raise the amount of insulin Mrs Jones was getting from 1 unit per hour to 2 units per hour to a total volume of 100 units.

Perhaps Mrs Jones had heard about the influx of doctors from the developing countries working in the Victoria Hospital. However, the morality of stripping doctors from developing countries to work in the First World was not on Mrs Jones's mind. In fact, nothing was on her mind. Slowly, her mind ceased to exist. Instead of Dr Kigali giving her 2 units per hour to a total of 100 units, he had kindly, although not deliberately, dialled up 100 units per hour to a total of 2000 units.

The Angel of Death poised in the corner of the ICU looked mirthfully across the room. 'I always win in the end,' he said as he and Mrs Jones skipped along the corridors of the hospital on their eternal journey home.

CHAPTER 3

At Mortality's Edge

Unfathomable Sea! whose waves are years,
Ocean of Time, whose waters of deep woe
Are brackish with the salt of human tears!
Thou shoreless flood, which in thy ebb and flow
Claspest the limits of mortality,
And sick of prey, yet howling on for more,
Vomitest thy wrecks on its inhospitable shore;
Treacherous in calm, and terrible in storm,
Who shall put forth on thee,
Unfathomable Sea?

'TIME' BY PERCY BYSSHE SHELLEY

One of the joys of the early years of residency is the opportunity to spend some time outside surgery. This was meant to produce a well-rounded surgeon who knew about medicine in its totality. For me, this opportunity came in my first year as a resident. I had successfully completed my internship and was now on the basic surgical scheme. I had not done much outside surgery in my internship, but now I felt the need to expand my horizons and learn a little about medicine in general.

Some resented the interruption to their surgical training. They saw the rotations to non-surgical terms as time spent not operating, wasted time. My first boss, Dr Agnes Perez, had always quoted Harvey Cushing's (the founder of modern neurosurgery) assertion, who said, 'Surgeons are physicians who operate', so I decided to take up the opportunity to do a non-surgical term. I had my choice of cardiology or immunology medicine. I opted for the latter.

It was during this term that I had the privilege of working with Dr Joseph Peterson and meeting the unforgettable Emma Kirby. She was seventeen.

Emma was referred by her family doctor from the rural township where she had been born. She had lived a tortured and difficult life and yet had maintained a dignity and courage that was beyond anything I had encounterd. At the age of ten, she witnessed her mother killed by her father during a domestic argument. The Department of Child Services was called and Emma was immediately admitted for examination after the incident. Along with a case of life-threatening pneumonia, she was also noted to have scratch marks around her thighs. Semen was collected from her vagina. The semen was matched to her father. Not only had her father left her with the emotional scars of abuse, but he had also left her with a viral illness whose manifestations were only beginning to be known at the time. It started initially with a cold that she could not shake. Antibiotics did not help. Colds progressed to atypical and rare pneumonias. Finally, Dr Peterson was called. She was fifteen when he diagnosed her with AIDS.

It was clear, even then, that Emma would not survive to see her twenty-first birthday. Slowly and inextricably, the complications of AIDS set in. At first, it was the various infections that she acquired. Then the tell-tale black lesions around her lips, Kaposi's Sarcomas. All the time, the medical community scratched its head for a cure, a control for a burgeoning epidemic that threatened society. So few knew what this awful virus meant and with the ignorance came an almost medieval reaction. Some surgeons demanded an AIDS test on almost every patient they operated on. Some even refused to operate, feeling that the disease was self-inflicted due to the reckless promiscuity associated with a gay lifestyle or the risks of sharing needles among intra-venous drug users. There was as much superstition about AIDS when it was first diagnosed as a disease as there was about the plague in the Middle Ages or leprosy, common even today in parts of the world.

For Emma, it was a disease that she had acquired through no deed of her own. She was a victim of paternal paedophilia and abuse – tragic manifestation of an evil far removed from what should be the joys of a childhood. She spent innumerable days in hospital as she went through the charade of primary school and then the first couple of years of high school. Her father had been arrested and jailed and in between hospital stays, she lived in a number of foster homes. Hospitals became life-saving for Emma in more ways than one. She befriended the nurses and the other patients and was always reluctant to go back to her foster home.

Dr Peterson had been there the whole time. He had organised the social workers, the foster home, the halfway house. He had organised the counselling. He had arranged the multiple antibiotics, treatments, steroids, intravenous lines, blood tests, arterial gas analyses; all a daily part of the life of an AIDS patient.

Joseph Peterson was one of the world's leading experts on this horrendous disease. He knew that a successful outcome in Emma's case was that she would die in her late teens instead of childhood.

Few doctors had Joe's compassionate dedication to his patients. He had decided that he was going to devote his life to this disease and its victims. When he was not in the ward alleviating the suffering of his patients he was in the research laboratory working on genetic research. He had no wife, no family, no children. His home was a one-bedroom flat near the hospital, but he was rarely there. Most of us who worked with him thought he lived in the hospital.

Emma was a girl who had seen more of life's anguish than was fair. When suffering is doled out to humanity it is not disbursed with equity, and Emma had received a dollop that, had it been shared among a hundred souls, would have been hard to bear. Yet despite her tragic life, her abuse, her illness, her lost childhood, her pain, her daily struggle to live, she smiled every day. Until today.

Emma Kirby had decided it was time to die. End-stage AIDS is an awful pathway to the afterlife, entailing recurrent infections and painful, disfiguring tumours. Emma had had enough. I was doing a round with Dr Peterson when she looked us both squarely in the face and announced her desire and intentions.

One night, I was at the nurse's desk still writing up medications for the new patients we had admitted during the day. Joseph Peterson arrived on the ward. I was surprised to see him.

'Is everyone OK?' he asked nonchalantly as he stared at the door to Room 4, Emma's room.

'Yeah, fine,' I replied. 'Do you want to do a ward round?' I could not believe he would be here for a social visit.

'No. I'm just going to see Emma.'

He walked towards her room and closed the door behind him. It was midnight. The surrounds were lit with the muted night-lights that gave all the familiar, ordinary objects cluttering the respirator ward an eerie, surreal existence, converting the scene into a Christmas grotto. The red LED lights flicked on and off, monitoring life. The green displays and the blue electric charger indicators added a pretty glow to walls that stand silent witnesses to one of the worst deaths that humans can endure – death by suffocation.

There were the lifelong smokers gasping for air through lungs that could hardly absorb sufficient oxygen to keep their owners in their mortal coil. There were end-stage lung cancer victims whose last days were to be spent drowning in blood gushing from vessels eaten away by the daily multiplying of murderous cells in their chest. There were old homeless men who had picked up pneumonia and were being pumped full of antibiotics and oxygen, fed, and then sent back out to their cardboard cubby-holes in the back alleys. Their ill-kept hair and disastrously soiled clothing were always a giveaway as to their predicament.

This was a joint ward shared between respiratory medicine and immunology. At the end of the ward was the collection of unfortunate souls who had contracted AIDS. Their food was served on disposable plates that were then incinerated lest the kitchen staff contract the virus. They were mostly gay men who had contracted the disease through unprotected sex, or they were intravenous drug users. Children like Emma were a rarity at a time when no one had heard of the term, 'AIDS baby'.

On our ward round that afternoon, she had looked at Joe beyond the oxygen mask that was now a permanent fixture over her face. Dark rings obscured her beauty. Her blonde hair, once in ponytails and tied with her characteristic powder-puff elastics, was now a tangled unwashed sprawl across the white hospital pillow.

'I do not want to live any more, Joey!' Even to say these words had been a monumental struggle for the girl. Her worldly possessions were on her bed and in the top drawer of her bedside cupboard were a brown Paddington bear, some underwear, a pair of jeans and a used cassette player that one of the nurses had given her. A big foil helium balloon was attached to the side of the bed railing, having been brought in by some acquaintances from the last halfway house in which she had lived. 'Get Well Soon' announced the balloon, an overly optimistic sentiment.

'Come on, Emma, we've been this bad before. The antibiotics are working and you'll be better soon.' Joseph Peterson did not like to give up. He had counselled patients whose fight had waned many times before. He knew the telltale signs of someone who's had enough, when a test needs to be delayed or when the pain of yet another blood gas analysis will tip the patient into giving up.

Emma was strong. He had not had to have this conversation with her before.

'I want to ... [*breath*] ... die. I've ... [*breath*] ... had enough.' There was no emotion in her voice. This was not a tantrum. This was not a manipulation for getting out of physiotherapy or her daily injections. Emma was dead serious.

I saw Joe leave her room deeply troubled. He had almost raised this girl. So many times she had given him a hug of gratitude when leaving the hospital after a lengthy stay. He sustained himself by those hugs. Joe sometimes plotted to adopt her. Once, he had brought himself to have a conversation with her social workers, but in the end he had never taken it any further.

Now, he quietly entered the room, hoping that Emma was asleep. He could hear the gasping. The door closed behind him. I continued to write notes but found myself imagining what was happening in there.

Emma would be on the bed, each breath laboured as if she was attempting to breathe with a gigantic stone atop her chest. Gasp, rest. Gasp, rest. Gasp.

She had had so many intravenous lines that all her peripheral veins had clotted. The only way to get antibiotics into Emma was through a central line, a tube that was placed just beneath her clavicle on the front of her chest and went straight into the larger veins around the heart. This meant she no longer needed to have her skin breached each time an injection was required. Unfortunately, this line needed to be replaced every ten days, a painful and uncomfortable procedure. It was a last-ditch effort. For Emma, it was to be a last measure.

Emma was awake. She had been waiting for Joe to come.

'Give . . . [breath] . . . it.' She was struggling but determined.

Joseph Peterson took out a vial of oral morphine and emptied it into a medication cup. Morphine would help to ease her pain and make her more comfortable. Morphine could also suppress her breathing. There was a minute and delicate balance between alleviating her pain and suppressing what little breathing capacity this young woman had remaining. She no longer cared. She wanted the anguish to stop.

He placed the vial before her. Emma was watching every movement. He looked at her and tears ran down his face.

'Please help me take it.' She was so weak that even bringing the small amount of fluid to her mouth was more effort than she could muster.

'I can't,' he said.

Her right hand came up slowly and grabbed the cup with a great but determined effort. She brought it to her lips and threw her head back to swallow the morphine with one gulp. She fell back to the bed.

Joe bent down and hugged her with all the longing and love that he had felt throughout her life as his patient. When he let go of her body, he sat down on the chair next to her bed and held her hand. The pulse oximeter attached to her ear read out the level of oxygen in her blood.

'Ninety per cent . . . 85 per cent . . . 60 per cent.' Emma's heart stopped, and with it, her pain, her struggle, her hope, her life.

At 2 am the night-shift nurse flung the door open. Joe looked up, startled. He had fallen asleep holding Emma's hand.

'Don't bother. She's gone,' he told the nurse.

'Do you want me to call her next of kin?' The nurse knew Dr Joseph Peterson only through his reputation as a compassionate doctor and her respect for him was first-hand. He had stayed with a patient who was dying, comforting her. She would have no reason to suspect him of any wrong doing. Emma was on the critical list and her death was not unexpected. He had done nothing wrong anyway. He had provided painkillers to alleviate the suffering.

'She doesn't have any next of kin. Just call the undertaker.' Joe got up and left.

Two days later, a handful of people gathered around her grave, including Emma's social worker. Dr Peterson told me he had placed a bunch of daisies on her headstone. She was buried next to her mother. Her father had already died in jail and had been cremated. She had no other family. The social worker and the priest stood quietly. Joe read the eulogy.

The only words he could muster were: 'She was the bravest and most beautiful person I have ever met.'

He continued to visit Emma Kirby's grave. Occasionally I went with him. He would just stand there and stare, tend to the flowers that grew nearby, or sometimes he would just mutter.

A few years later, retroviral drugs arrested the development of AIDS and the disease was controllable for the vast majority of patients. We came to understand its transmission through blood and the reaction to AIDS, as a disease, became more humane and less ignorant.

I remember seeing Peterson around this time.

'Did you read the article in the *New England Journal of Medicine*? They are getting good results from these new retrovirals they have developed.'

He looked at me, watching my reaction closely with those intense scientific eyes. I knew immediately what was on his mind.

Joseph Peterson gave up clinical medicine a year later to concentrate purely on research. He had committed the greatest crime a doctor could.

He cared too much.

CHAPTER 4

The Power to Hurt

They that have power to hurt and will do none,
That do not do the thing they most do show,
Who moving others are themselves as stone,
Unmoved, cold, and to temptation slow –
They rightly do inherit heaven's graces,
And husband nature's riches from expense;
They are the lords and owners of their faces,
Others but stewards of their excellence.
The summer's flower is to the summer sweet,
Though to itself it only live and die;
But if that flower with base infection meet,
The basest weed outbraves his dignity;
For sweetest things turn sourest by their deeds:
Lilies that fester smell far worse than weeds.

'SONNET 94' BY WILLIAM SHAKESPEARE

It was a relief to be back in a surgical rotation after the immunology term. I was back in my comfort zone and enjoying being in theatres again. I hated the pills and potions of medicine. Give me a knife any day. I had one more term to go to complete my first year of basic surgical training, and one last hurdle before the calendar flipped me to the next year and another level of seniority. That hurdle was Phillip Nordstrom.

Mr Phillip Nordstrom was a great surgeon. He was the elite. He was one of the few surgeons who insisted on being called Mister and not Doctor, a tradition that originated back in the Middle Ages. To become a surgeon in those days – in fact, up until the eighteenth century – you did not do a medical degree. Rather, you trained as a barber. Physicians first did medical degrees and hence were called doctor. But, so proud were early surgeons of their barber ancestry that even after the rules had changed – the colleges were formed and surgeons had to go to medical school first – they preserved the tradition of calling themselves by the appellation Mister.

Mr Nordstrom's surgical skills were legendary. As a result of these skills and his habit of not speaking unless it was absolutely necessary, he commanded great respect and had a presence that somehow filled anyone who worked with him with awe. His registrars toed the line with considerable care lest they end up on the receiving end of a sharp tongue that could almost tattoo their skin.

I was in my first year of basic surgical training when I first encountered Phillip Nordstrom. All surgical trainees and residents knew that one good word from him, one recommendation, would completely alter their career trajectory for the better. Doors would open and jobs would be made available. Positions could be created if need be.

To get an advanced surgical training position, you need to have a clean record and a mentor during the three years of basic surgical training after medical school, when the slightest slip-up, carelessness, misdiagnosis or personality flaw is noted. Each day brings with it multiple opportunities to make mistakes and few opportunities to shine. Making sure that the positive outweighs the negative is the best you hope for. At the end of that time, interviews are held for senior training positions, so-called 'accredited positions'. These interviews decide whether the doctor, who by now has been out of high school for between eight and ten years, is suitable for further training to become a surgeon, or whether they need another year or two in basic surgical training. Fifteen surgeons sit on the interview committee, deciding the fate of all these doctors. Only one or two are admitted to the exclusive club of accredited surgical trainees.

A bad word from Phillip Nordstrom meant you might as well plan on a career as a rural general practitioner. The worse the opinion held of the trainee, the more remote the rural posting. I still had two more years of basic surgical training and could not afford not to impress Nordstrom. It was best to regard the hospital as an extension of home. The hospital was where I slept, ate, played and worked – a life outside did not exist for me.

*

Rumours about the power of some senior surgeons were rife but could never be substantiated. One young trainee was rotated to the term of a notoriously harsh supervisor. He asked for two weeks' leave for personal reasons before starting the term. He was told, 'Sure.' However, at the end of the year, the young trainee was not reappointed to the hospital, despite multiple protests from other doctors. He was last heard of on the Emergency Physician training program – in those days this was where rejects from the surgical training program ended up.

This absolute power over young doctors was all around. Another young training candidate had been given super-lative references by his surgical supervisor, whom he'd used as a referee. However, the supervisor rang the chairman of the selection committee and, in addition to telling him how wonderful the young Chinese candidate was, told him he worried about the applicant's long-term dedication to surgery and cited inferior communication skills. The young doctor was not appointed to the surgical training program. It was an effective way to exclude someone from the club but was it a clear-cut case of racial discrimination? It was a source of much debate but once again, making a concrete case for such allegations is next to impossible unless there is undisputed evidence, such as a witness to the behaviour, and even then how many will jeopardise their career and come forwards? For the most part, accusations of discrimination remained whispers and heresy.

One examiner for the College of Surgeons was rumoured to have asked a trainee a question about the embryology of the spleen. This was something that was rarely asked in an examination. The trainee looked at him painfully. 'That is a hard question, sir,' he said respectfully.

'This is a hard exam, son,' was the reply. The trainee failed.

*

My rotation under Mr Phillip Nordstrom exposed me to his robust training methods as well as his undisputable genius.

A 70-year-old man came in to casualty having fallen from a ladder about six days prior. I reviewed him, examined his chest and arranged an x-ray because of some pain around his lower ribs on the right side. The x-ray showed that there was slight shadowing in the base of the chest but nothing convincing. My view was that the patient could be sent home.

I rang Nordstrom, who was on call. I described the case in detail and with clinical precision, then indicated my conclusion that the patient should be sent home, to be reviewed within a week.

'Put a chest tube into him!' was the reply, then silence. He had hung up on me.

A chest tube is a device used to drain fluid or air from the chest cavity – a large bore plastic tube connected to an underwater sealed bottle. Putting one into a patient is not a minor undertaking. It requires local anaesthetic, calculating the precise position to make a finger's-breadth incision, followed by considerable pushing and tearing of the muscles between the ribs until one finger has made its way into the chest cavity. Then, the tube is inserted blind in the hope that it does not perforate the lungs, liver or even the heart, which is situated not too far away from the skin where the incision is made. Harrowing for the first-timer, even with supervision.

I had never put a chest tube in before, however I knew the theory. I went up to the Cardiac ICU to see if I could find a senior registrar to give me a hand. It was 7 pm and I had finished my shift at 5 pm. I was simply seeing the patient to take the load off the night registrar, but now I was stuck. I did not feel I could hand this over.

ICU was full that night. A range of patients who had had cardiac bypass procedures that day lined the open ward, each with a large monitor pronouncing them alive and with tubes extruding from their chests and their mouths – respirators and drains.

I remember the instructions given to me when I did my first shift in ICU. The registrar on-call took me over to the end of one of the beds. Each patient had a large piece of printed cardboard on which the nurse looking after them charted hourly readings of their vital signs, blood pressure, pulse rate, urine output and the like. The registrar told me, 'Look out for gradients. Gradients are bad.'

It was the best advice anyone had ever given to me and it has stood the test of time throughout my medical life. A falling blood pressure might indicate cardiac failure: it is a gradient, and hence bad. A rising pulse rate might indicate hidden bleeding: once again, a gradient, and hence bad. All gradients are bad. Falling urine output. Rising temperature. Falling oxygen levels. All bad.

Tonight, the registrar in ICU was Dr Wing Li. He was adjusting a patient's medication. He looked up casually at the chest x-ray and said, 'I definitely wouldn't put a tube in this one. Who told you to do that?'

'Mr Nordstrom,' I replied timidly.

'Look, give me ten minutes and I'll come down and see the patient for you.' This was a brave call – he was setting himself up to contradict God.

I was grateful that I could pass this case off to a more senior doctor. I was feeling way out of my depth. I could not understand why Nordstrom would nonchalantly instruct me to do a procedure that I had never done and, even so, was one that was not normally performed unsupervised until the second or third year on the training program.

Dr Li walked in to see the patient with me. He got out his stethoscope and was about to examine him when the curtains around the cubicle were pushed apart. It was Phillip Nordstrom doing the evening round. There were seven residents and twelve medical students behind him.

'What's going on?' he said, pinning me to the wall with his glare.

'I asked Dr Li to give me a hand, sir. I needed his opinion. . . I . . . I have never put in . . .' I stopped talking. He had his forefinger up and was motioning me out of the cubicle.

'Did you ring me earlier to ask me my opinion?' He was shouting at the top of his voice in the middle of casualty.

'Yes, sir, I did.' I was blushing. I hated it when I blushed. It was a sign of weakness.

'Did I or did I not give you my opinion?' He was cool but unforgiving.

'Yes, sir, you did.' I was feeling weak in the knees now. I could see a fellow resident standing behind Nordstrom smiling. We were rivals who would eventually compete head-to-head for the same advanced surgical training job. He obviously felt he now had the upper hand.

'Then why have you asked assistance from Dr [sarcastically] Wing F-u-c-k-i-n-g Li?'

This time I did not get a chance to respond.

'Go and put a chest tube in that f-u-c-k-i-n-g man's fucking chest, *fucking now!*'

There was no clearer directive given in the history of mankind. There were no ambiguities. My rival resident was now openly smirking. Phillip Nordstrom had already turned and the caravan was gathering speed out of Casualty behind him.

I turned back to re-enter the cubicle. I did not want to look at any other human beings for this and the next lifetime if possible. I was almost in tears. Dr Wing Li had disappeared from the side of the cubicle. Few were brave before the full force of Mr Phillip Nordstrom's ire.

I looked round to see one of the nurses opening up the chest-tube insertion pack.

'I'll get this ready for you while you wash your hands.' She was patching me up and knew I needed help. God bless nurses when they are on your side.

I went to the sink, composed myself by throwing copious amounts of water on my face, and then scrubbed. When I re-entered the cubicle, my gown and gloves and all the instruments I needed were waiting for me. She was a saint, this nurse.

I explained to the patient what I was about to do. My explanation did not alleviate his considerable anxiety: he had heard the entire interaction between Nordstrom and myself and had probably come to the conclusion that perhaps this was the first time I had seen a patient, let alone put a chest tube in. I maintained a semblance of composure.

I then prepped the skin with alcohol, found the spot between the fourth and fifth rib and injected some local anaesthetic. I made a two-centimetre incision and inserted a pair of forceps in between the ribs to make an opening into the chest so that I could insert a tube about 1.5 centimetres in diameter – enough to drain any blood or air that was in the chest. Nordstrom was as convinced as I was not that the patient had a chest full of blood from the trauma of falling off the ladder.

My forceps went in with considerable force before I was finally able to hear the hiss of air escaping from the chest. I placed my forefinger into the hole I had made and followed it in with the chest tube on the end of the forceps. Once the tube was securely in, to the depth marked on the side, I sewed it in with a silk stitch to secure it. The patient had not said a word during what must have been a painfully uncomfortable procedure.

Now the moment of truth. Was Nordstrom correct, or was I? I unclamped the chest tube. A gush of blood under high pressure came out of the tube, hitting me in the chest and falling onto my shoes and the floor. It was startling and dramatic. Nordstrom was right. How had he known?

However, the blood did not stop flowing. I quickly connected the end of the chest tube to the suction bottle at my feet to avoid any more spillage. One litre. Two litres. Two and a half litres.

I suddenly went pale and weak at the knees. Surely, the only thing that could explain this level of bleeding was that I had placed the tube into the right ventricle of the heart. If this was true, it was almost certainly fatal. I could have just killed this man. Panic hit my very soul. I immediately reached for a syringe and drew 20 millilitres of blood from his arm.

'Urgent cross-match please!' I handed it to the nurse.

I barked orders for an urgent chest x-ray. Meanwhile, I watched the patient, who miraculously was unperturbed. He was still breathing, pulse rate unchanged, blood pressure not falling. No gradients. It seemed an eternity until the portable x-ray machine and attendant arrived, and another as they went through the motions: wait as they plug the machine into the wall socket; wait as they place the film behind the patient in the bed; wait until they crank up the bed; wait until they call 'x-ray' so that others can escape the radiation.

Then, click. Now wait until the films are processed.

At long last, the films – those grey and white tellers of fortunes – came out of the processor. There was no doubt about it, the tube overlapped the heart. It could well be in the heart. I panicked further.

I ran up to ICU with the x-ray, leaving the Casualty senior resident with the patient. Dr Li was there. I explained the situation. His only solution was to ring Mr Nordstrom and ask his advice. He did not want to get into more trouble.

'Mr Nordstrom, I am sorry to disturb you again, sir . . .' I stammered out the entire story and my exact procedure. He was silent until I'd finished, when he pronounced, 'Fuck! Get a CT scan!' This was the only advice I got.

By midnight the CT scan had been done. It showed that the tube was in perfect position and was nowhere near the heart. The chest x-ray had reflected only a two-dimensional view of the chest. My tube was behind the heart and not in it.

I rang Phillip Nordstrom to report the findings and to report that the patient had drained a full four litres of blood from his chest and was feeling the best he had felt for a week. I was feeling the worst I had felt since I could remember.

Nordstrom listened in silence and then asked, 'Have you learned anything tonight, son?'

'Yes, sir, I have learned never to doubt you'.

'Tonight has taught me something too, son. It has taught me that you care.' He hung up.

*

Nordstrom was tough but, fundamentally, he was a good surgeon and a good man. However, in a very few cases a doctor's power over registrars and residents seemed to be a source of personal satisfaction. One such surgeon's cruelty to registrars was matched only by the thrall he had over students wishing to specialise in his area. He stimulated great resentment and fear among his juniors and colleagues, and he controlled their futures with the same disdain as one might spray a fly with insecticide.

Late in his career his operating, which had been exemplary, started to deteriorate, and some of his patients began to suffer adverse outcomes. The nurses on the wards noticed it first. They would report it to his colleagues, who'd say, 'He's just going through a bad patch.' No one really wanted to take the man on.

His colleagues sat in on morbidity and mortality meetings where his results were presented. His name came up constantly for the sheer number of complications his cases were presenting. Finally, one day, the nurses ran to get the surgeon who was operating next door.

'Please come, quickly!'

There, in the middle of the operating theatre, stood this notorious surgeon with his theatre scrubs around his ankles; he was urinating in a corner. An orderly had been called to help him get his pants on and the surgeon called him a 'sick fuck'. It seemed that he had gone stark raving mad.

His wife was called. He was sedated and admitted to the hospital immediately. Within two hours a head scan was done, which showed that he had a frontal brain tumour the size of a grapefruit, and it was inoperable. He was a dead man walking. His abnormal behaviour, his extreme rudeness and the complications that had arisen after some of his operations were ascribed to his sickness.

Sometime after this I was visiting the ward where he was a patient, catching up on some notes I had to write up. I had heard he'd been admitted and was strangely curious to see him, so I used the notes as an excuse. He was standing in the middle of the ward, pyjamas on, and struggling with his robe, trying to get his leg into its sleeve.

'I must have gained weight or something – this robe fitted me fine last week!' He was ridiculously inappropriate – the tumour had destroyed his spatial abilities as well as his inhibition. A resident was attempting to get him back to bed and to help him straighten out his robe. The great man looked over towards me and called me over. We went back to his room together – I think the resident was relieved someone else could baby-sit for a while.

'They reckon I'm going to die.'

I didn't know what to say. I reached out and placed my hand on his shoulder.

'I've been a bit of a bastard, haven't I? There'll be a lot of people happy to see me like this. Fuck them. I wouldn't do it any differently, you know. Fuck them. One of the problems with this disease in my head is that I can't dress myself.' He looked at me intensely and he began to cry. I stood up and hugged his head as he sobbed uncontrollably. Then I smelt a familiar smell. He was wetting himself without any awareness.

The terror of the wards, the maker and breaker of careers, was defeated and humiliated. Three days after that he died in the hospital to which he had dedicated so much of his life.

His funeral was attended by only a handful of people. The overwhelming sentiment in the hospital was that he had got what was coming to him. I disagreed. The man was a great loss to surgery. He could certainly be cruel, but his manner was cruel because he was a breed of surgeon whose only way of showing kindness was to perform a good operation. It was through countless lives saved, through multiple cancers removed (which had been deemed by those less skilled as inoperable) and through a complication rate that had for years been so low as to be incredible, that this surgeon had expressed his love for humanity. He was not a man who stood for fools, nor was he easy to like or admire. However, as a surgeon he was no less than Leonardo da Vinci. Just as the extremes of genius are often mistaken for madness, so was this man's eventually intensely antisocial behaviour taken to be deliberate. It was not, as we had eventually found out – but too late to save him.

Society dictates that surgeons have to be nice as well as competent. In fact, surgeons who are nice but incompetent generally have bigger practices than those who are extremely skilful, but rude or objectionable. Patients are sometimes like children who develop a complex because one or both parents is out at work all the time. They interpret the lack of time given to them as a lack of love or care. To the parent, his or her way of showing care to the family is to ensure that the rent is paid and that there is food on the table. The extra two jobs that rob a child of his parents' presence are a way of saying, 'I love you. You are cared for.' This was how some surgeons showed their compassion to their patients and trainees. Not by kind words of encouragement, but by healing with steel and by training their residents to do the same with skill and discipline.

As a resident in the hospital, I did not have the luxury of time – the time to spend with a patient exploring their life, their ambitions, their inner fears. I too showed my care by making sure my tasks were done to keep them alive. Perhaps many interpreted that as a lack of compassion. But why else be a surgeon, if not to look after humanity? A profound duty of care is our lot.

I was competent. The best I mustered in addition to competence was to be civil to my patients, sometimes despite days without sleep. Yet, years later, when I tasted illness myself, I too craved for compassion more than competence. Illogical but true.

For the surgeons who had once terrified us all so much, competence was enough.

CHAPTER 5
To Sleep

A flock of sheep that leisurely pass by
One after one; the sound of rain, and bees
Murmuring; the fall of rivers, winds and seas,
Smooth fields, white sheets of water, and pure sky;
I've thought of all by turns, and still I lie
Sleepless; and soon the small birds' melodies
Must hear, first uttered from my orchard trees,
And the first cuckoo's melancholy cry.
Even thus last night, and two nights more I lay,
And could not win thee, Sleep! by any stealth:
So do not let me wear tonight away:
Without Thee what is all the morning's wealth?
Come, blessed barrier between day and day,
Dear mother of fresh thoughts and joyous health!

'TO SLEEP' BY WILLIAM WORDSWORTH

The weekend resident surgery shift at the Victoria Hospital lasted just that – the weekend. The surgical residents were on a one-in-two shift in those days. One worked the week, averaging 12–16 hours each day and over 80 hours of work during the weeks when you were on call. Either you were on call or the other resident allotted to the same term was on call. The blur between work and 'not work' seemed to fade even more and you were constantly tuned into your ever-present companion, the beeper.

The residents of previous years had discovered a small cupboard in the respiratory lab where someone had set up a camp-bed. Unfortunately, we shared the room with the blood gas analysis machine.

Whirr, whirr, whirr, beep, tush, tush, tush, dit dit dit dit dit . . .

It lasted perhaps ten seconds, but it was long enough to wake the dead. Every ten minutes it sprang to life, calibrating its measures and printing out a report on a dot-matrix printer. The noise cut through the night and pierced your existence. The machine seemed to have a life of its own and, having been stuck in the cupboard all its life, was vengeful. Its sole aim, apart from predicting life and death among the patients whose blood it analysed, was to keep any resident who thought they could catch a few minutes' sleep during their marathon shift from doing so.

I had gone around the wards making sure every last request from the night-shift nurses had been attended to: Panadol for bed 4, a sleeping tablet for bed 6. Bed 9 needed his first dose of antibiotics and it had to be given by a doctor. By the end of the first day there was inevitably a dull ache in my knees that often gave way to shin splints and then shot straight up into hip pain.

Migraines were a common occurrence for me and I would be constantly popping anti-migraine tablets. By midnight even the smallest request seemed immensely tedious. No brain power was required for most of a resident's work, so it was possible to keep going on and on, from charting tablets to admitting patients to the ward, from giving the first dose of antibiotics to pronouncing people dead. It was all stuff that could be done by the brain-dead, which was what we became after the first 36 hours of our shift.

Nurses could make life hell or heaven. If you had a shift of experienced and sensible nurses then life was easy. The alternative was the nurse straight out of university, who saw herself as the custodian of quality, the barometer of good care in our hospital system. The majority of these nurses were bureaucrats rather than carers. These nurses were the new breed, the norm.

In the old days, nurses trained in the hospital. They had breaks to rapidly imbibe theoretical knowledge, then returned to the hospital to learn from the best educational system that man has invented – workplace training. They learned and absorbed from those with more experience and more skill. Slowly, they taught others with less skill and experience. By the time they graduated they had seen a lot of illness and health and certainly knew what a nurse does for a living.

In today's university nursing educational scheme, the nurse spends a lot of time being taught to be compassionate (as if this is a skill that can be taught). They do a multitude of role-playing activities and video each other in simulated patient interactions. They study behavioural sciences, pharmacology, anatomy, physiology, biochemistry and come out knowing very little about what it is to be a nurse in the truest sense of the word.

They are told that they, the nurse, are the controller of quality. No one tells them that they are actually the difference between life and death for some patients. The hospital-trained nurses knew that making a bed without creases meant bedsores were minimised. Bedsores could turn into terrible and painful infections. University nurses feel it is beneath them to make beds. Walk into any hospital and you are likely to see patients or their relatives making beds. The hospital-trained nurses knew that rolling a patient over, washing them thoroughly, cutting their toenails, feeding them and caring for their wounds prevented complications that could result in significant morbidity or death. Many university nurses feel that filling out the latest quality-assurance survey, making sure the notes are up-to-date and taking their breaks on time are paramount.

All they need to know, and what university does not teach them, is that patients are 'nursed' not 'doctored' back to good health.

It is no secret that the experienced, hospital-trained nurses in theatres are life-saving to both the trainee surgeon and the patient. There is nothing so lonely as operating in the middle of the night when you are slightly uncomfortable and yet do not want to disturb the sleep of the specialist in charge. The experienced nurses help you.

'Doctor Jackson usually uses a figure-of-eight stitch for this closure,' they might say with a knowing look.

They sense your discomfort, but having seen it in a hundred trainees before you, know that you will turn out all right with a little help here and there.

Many university nurses cannot wait for the operation to be over to fill out their incident forms. 'The registrar delayed the procedure unnecessarily because he did not know which stitch to use.' You then have to write a report to explain yourself.

*

Thelma Ward was a 77-year-old lady on Ward 8. Unable to feed herself, she was losing significant weight. She had had a valve replacement, during which a clot had entered her brain circulation and killed off the parts of her brain that allowed her to speak and to move her arms with sufficient coordination to bring food to her mouth. Each day I would see Thelma on my rounds, and each day I would pass the nutrition team, who were contemplating putting a tube into her subclavian vein and feeding her artificially with nutritional fluids. All she needed was a nurse to help her eat her food. They were too busy filling out forms.

One day I saw volunteers on our ward. I asked one of them to go and feed Thelma. From then on, each day at mealtime, one of the Pink Ladies (our blessed hospital volunteers) would arrive and feed Thelma. She started gaining weight and became less confused. She was discharged to a nursing home where she would spend the rest of her life.

Some nurses could be absolutely pitiless. Ward rounds used to be a collective effort where the nurses and doctors worked as an integral part of the healthcare team, sharing information about patients and determining the best course of action for an individual. The charge nurse knew everything about the patients – how they had slept, their overnight temperature, the fact that their cousin had visited yesterday, who was the first family member they had seen, that the skin on their buttock was slightly red and needed examination.

Most university nurses see ward rounds as an unnecessary part of their day's activities. Walk into any ward today and ask the nurse sitting behind the counter about a patient's condition. They are unlikely to know. The nurse looking after the patient is on a break, the notes are in the treatment bay, the patient is not in the ward and they do not know where she is.

A compounding problem to this disastrous and failed experiment in nursing education is the system of promotion for nurses in hospitals today. The only way for a nurse to progress in status and pay is to be promoted to administration. Take a really good clinical nurse. How does the health system reward her? It makes her part of the clipboard brigade.

One of the most tragic events I remember in the Victoria Hospital was seeing a great clinical nurse promoted to assistant director of nursing. One night, as I left the hospital through the back entrance, I glanced across at a lit office. There was Sister Pauline Cromwell in her newly acquired office, entering patient occupancy figures into a spreadsheet on the computer. What a waste.

Of course, there are still those nurses who take pride in their work and the care of patients, but their efforts can get lost in a sea of mediocrity and buck-passing.

*

Whirr, whirr, whirr, beep, tush, tush, tush, dit dit dit dit dit . . .

I was still trying to sleep. If only I could just have ten minutes, perhaps my headache would go. I'd already had more Panadeine today than was safe by any human measure.

My left eye felt like it was bursting. I had not slept for over two days.

Please God, let me sleep.

My beeper went again. Ward 6. God . . . there was a university nurse in charge tonight.

I roused and walked up the stairs and across the bridge connecting Building 5 to the Albert Building. Ward 6 was where the neurosurgical patients were. Many of us in the hospital called it the vege-patch. This was where the long-term comatose patients spent their days being cared for and kept alive despite the fact that their chance of recovery was nil.

Bed after bed of bodies who used to be mothers, fathers, sisters, girlfriends, football heroes were now bedridden, lying in strange and unnatural postures, arms contorted in the classic extended finger and thumb pose with the wrist and the elbow bent. Eyes closed.

Mason Smith, a 26-year-old former athlete and legendary womaniser, had had his brain tumour excised neatly. Along with the tumour, his speech, his consciousness, his personality, his mind and his thoughts had also been neatly excised, and now he was in the vegetable patch.

Often, when I visited this ward, I thought of the argument between those who felt that thought was a product of simple biochemical processes in the brain and those who believed in an ephemeral, untouchable mind. An afternoon spent here would go a long way in settling the debate once and for all. Destroy the brain and you destroy the person. Descartes' assertion '*Cogito ergo sum*' (I think therefore I am) should be replaced with, 'No one has touched my brain, hence I exist'. Cut the wrong bits of the brain out and you get a human being where the lights are on, but there is no one at home.

Mason was running a temperature. The nurse looking after him was one of the new breed of nurses who was more interested in the paperwork to be filled out than the patients to be cared for. All she wanted was to be able to put in her notes, 'Resident aware'. That cleared her of any medico-legal liability in case this blew up into a more complicated situation. It is far more important in these days of medical litigation to ensure that your back is protected before providing quality care. Making sure the paper trail was complete was, for her, more important than taking responsibility for any decisions. Mason's temperature had been up and down for days now, but she had just finished her observation round and it was best to report the abnormality, again, to the resident. This way, the resident took responsibility and she could go on her tea break.

I examined Mason by the book. I suctioned out some phlegm from his throat and sent it off for pathology culture. The fluid would be spread onto a plate of nutrients and then placed in a warm oven for a day to see if bacteria grew. If it did we'd determine what type of bacteria and which antibiotic would be best to cure them.

I filled out all the forms and took the blood. His cubital fossa, the bend in his elbow where the veins were prominent and where blood was usually drawn from, was impossible to get to, so I needed to do a femoral vein tap. The femoral vein is the large vein that passes through the front of the groin and the next easiest place in the human body to get to with a needle to draw blood.

I undressed Mason, felt the point halfway between his pubic bone and the tip of his hip and plunged my needle into the skin, upright. I was straight in. Of course Mason did not react. He gave no indication of pain. His brain was too destroyed to monitor a minor infraction upon his body. I took 20 millilitres of blood and then asked the nurse to put pressure on the site while I emptied the blood into various tubes in measured amounts and labelled each. I looked up to see her leaving the cubicle.

'Sorry, I'm on break now,' she said from behind the curtain.

I reached across and put pressure on the femoral vein before we ended up with a bruise the size of his thigh. This is the problem with taking blood from this vein – it continues to bleed unless pressure is applied. Ten minutes by the clock. All I could hear was the sound of the various vegetables breathing, most with the assistance of ventilators.

I cleaned up and put the sharps away. Along with the blood I collected a urine sample and both sent for cultures and a pathology screen. Finally, I arranged a chest x-ray. This was the standard septic screen. A temperature is indicative of an infection. The infection is most commonly in the chest, urine, wound or blood, so the idea is to screen the lot. As the tubes made their way to the lab, I made my way back to the small cupboard in the respiratory lab to try to rest.

Whirr, whirr, whirr, beep, tush, tush, tush, dit dit dit dit dit . . .

I tried so hard to sleep. Eyes closed. Meditation. Counting sheep. My beeper went again. I phoned the ward.

'Could you please come back and write up the notes about Mason Smith. You didn't write down what you did.' It was the nurse from hell, just back from her break.

'I will do it in the morning,' I said, and hung up.

Maybe I should just give up trying to sleep. I lay down on the camp-bed again. Through the small window up high, a red glow shone. It was the sign on the front of the Emergency Department, a huge red cross in neon lights: 'We are open. Come to us with your injuries and illnesses, your excesses and your stupidities. We will do our best to heal you and get you back to your drinking and smoking next week.'

I closed my eyes. My head now felt as though it was about to blow up.

Whirr, whirr, whirr, beep, tush, tush, tush, dit dit dit dit dit . . .

When was the last time I had urinated? I could not remember. I really had not drunk or eaten for some time now. The cost-cutting measures in the hospital included the biscuits and cordial we used to have in theatres. You had always been able to rely on coming out of theatre and at least having a biscuit and a drink of cordial, even toast.

Between 4 and 5 am your body's steroid levels are at their lowest. I always craved for toast then. Now, all one could have was the soft drinks and the packets of chips from the vending machines at the front of the hospital. If you had the exact change then you had a meal of salt and vinegar chips and a Coke. No change, no food.

The cafeteria opened at 6 am.

I thought of my boss, the specialist in charge. He was sleeping soundly at home. I could not resent him for that, he had paid his dues. He too had lain on this same bed some years previously. He would always boast about how much worse it was for him than for the residents and registrars today. I found it hard to believe. I just wanted to sleep. Please God, let me have some sleep.

Whirr, whirr, whirr, beep, tush, tush, tush, dit dit dit dit dit . . .

My beeper went off again. 'Code Blue, Ward 17, Code Blue, Ward 17.' I got up and ran.

Ward 17 was the vascular ward. Mrs Latitia Monty had had a vein graft to her groin to bridge the gap between a blocked femoral artery and the rest of her leg circulation. This had been done a week ago and Latitia was due to be discharged later today. Five minutes ago, her vein graft had disintegrated and her femoral artery was emptying its contents of high-pressured blood into her groin. The metal clips that held her skin together were giving way and Latitia Monty had now become a monstrous fountain of gushing blood spurting up to the ceiling. I walked in to see the nurse placing towels around the groin.

'Put some pressure on the groin, for God's sake!' I called out. The nurse looked at me, startled. Mrs Latitia Monty was amazingly calm.

I reached across and put my bare palm on the bleeding. Blood was oozing between my fingers, but it slowed the gushing.

'Call theatre and tell them we need to come up. Call the anaesthetic registrar. Who is the consultant? Call the blood bank and tell them we need some blood. Is there any already cross-matched? Get me the night intern.' This lady could die in the next three minutes if her bleeding was left unchecked.

I looked up at Latitia. Between her and certain death stood the pressure from my palm. She was in a lot of pain because of the pressure on her open wound but she mustered a smile.

'I knew it wouldn't go right, Doctor. I just had a feeling something was going to happen.'

'It will be OK, ma'am. We can fix this. I know you are in a lot of pain, but just bear with me.' I tried to be reassuring.

'You do what you need to do, Doctor.' She seemed resigned to her fate.

The challenge was to transport her to theatre with me hanging on to her groin. The only way was for me to jump up on the trolley and straddle her while the whole bed was wheeled to theatre.

There was blood all over the bed as I straddled the patient, my hands pressed firmly on her groin. Slowly, the bed was moved down the corridor – it must have been a macabre scene. A nurse was trying to place a blanket on Latitia as we moved to allow her some modesty on the long trip down the corridor, across the landing and during the eternal wait for the lift to theatres. The slightest movement caused blood to gush. I had to keep absolutely still, so the lift was difficult to enter as the orderlies tried to negotiate this hideous combination of blood-drenched patient and doctor into it. Several people were waiting, but decided to let us through first. A wise move. Finally, we all made it up to theatre and into an operating room.

The anaesthetic registrar was standing by. She injected her drugs. Latitia was now pain-free, soundly asleep. The registrar intubated her and started the ventilation. Dr Smith, the vascular surgeon, arrived on the scene.

'Keep the fucking pressure on until we're ready!' he shouted, as if I needed to be told. He went into the scrub bay. The nurses had already started laying out the instruments. I was not sterile, but at times like this all convention goes out of the window. There was no time now for the luxury of sterility, the bleeding had to be brought under control immediately. We would sanitise the wound after I was able to let go of this poor woman's groin.

Smith walked back in. He called out for a vascular clamp.

'OK, let go slowly,' he called to me, clamp in hand. I slowly removed the pressure. The gushing blood hit me square in the face. As I got off the trolley, he tore open the wound with clip removers and was about to apply the vascular clamp. Blood arrived from the blood bank and the anaesthetist hung up the first bag.

'We have it!' Smith shouted. 'OK. Surgical prep now!'

'Hey,' he called to me. 'Go get scrubbed and give me a hand!'

I washed my face, scrubbed and came back in for the four-hour procedure to reconstruct Latitia's groin and her leg circulation.

'I've been trying out these new vein grafts recently but I don't think it's an effective technique,' Smith said, as he put the last stitch into the new Gore-Tex graft. I said nothing. As a reward for assisting him, I was allowed to close the wound. Any operating is better than no operating.

Surgical progress is built on successes and failures. New operations have to be tried or else we learn nothing. However, sometimes they do not work. Sometimes patients die so that others might live from the mistakes that inform and teach. Surgical experimentation is an absolute necessity. For the most part, it is minor experimentation. It is about trying a new stitch, or a new incision or a small variation on what has been done before. Sometimes, it is about trying a whole new approach to an operation.

An ethics committee governs brand-new techniques. New treatments, new operations, surveys, requests for patient information, all go through the hospital ethics committee. Most hospitals have one. These committees are usually made up of hospital administrators, lawyers, priests, lay people and, finally, politicians. Most ethics committees take their role of protecting patients seriously; however, some members set unrealistically high protections for patients, so that they became obstructive.

Getting a research idea through an ethics committee is a difficult and time-consuming task. It is a wonder any research ever gets done. Yet, someone has to look after the patients' interests, and their role is vital. Hence, the battle between the experimenters and the ethics committees rages as a healthy, if not mutually frustrating, monthly tussle.

I wrote up my notes and prescribed some high-dose antibiotics for Latitia: infection was the major problem for her now. Her team would look after her. My job was done. Now what I needed more than anything was sleep. I went back to the cupboard. The blood gas analysis machine greeted me.

Whirr, whirr, whirr, beep, tush, tush, tush, dit dit dit dit dit . . .

Beep beep beep. My beeper had six messages on it. Ward 6 again.

'Yes, someone called me?' It was now about 9 am and the new shift of day nurses was in action.

'We have a message here from the night nurse that you have not written up one of the patients you saw last night – Mason.' The nurse was polite but assertive.

'I will come over shortly.'

I went back to pick up my stethoscope from the respiratory cupboard. The blood analysis machine was uttering its triumphant call.

Whirr, whirr, whirr, beep, tush, tush, tush, dit dit dit dit dit . . .

CHAPTER 6

Lucy

Whether at Naishapur or Babylon,
Whether the Cup with sweet or bitter run,
The Wine of Life keeps oozing drop by drop,
The Leaves of Life keep falling one by one.

THE RUBAIYYAT OF OMAR KHAYYAM, VIII

My beeper went off. Nothing new. It was someone in the main wards wanting me to chart some sleeping pills. The time was 10.30 pm. I was on call, again.

My beeper sounded yet again. I went to the ward to answer it.

'Yeah, Doctor Khadra here.'

'Mohamed, do you want to help with an appendix?' It was John Redman. He had become an attending medical officer at the hospital after his training. Ever since my intern rotation working three years previously, we had become friends. Despite the disparity in seniority and age, we seemed to get along and had had a number of golf games together and even a few dinners.

'I'll be right down.' I quickly charted the six or seven things the nurses had wanted and headed for the theatres. I wondered if I would be allowed to handle the scalpel. More than ever, I lived to operate. My logbook was growing steadily with a list of operations at which I was becoming familiar and competent. It was a far cry from that first operation, when John had been my registrar.

All surgical residents had to keep logbooks. They listed down the number and type of operations they had assisted in or, at best, actually conducted. There were columns where one ticked whether the resident had been an assistant or an operator and whether they were supervised directly or indirectly. The more operations listed in the logbook the happier I was and the greater the chance I might be allowed to do more complex procedures in the future. Each skill built on the last – it was an incremental educational system that had stood the test of time. The gut feeling of the supervising surgeon is still the best analysis of whether a resident is competent to take on a particular operation or not.

I ran into the scrub bay to change into my theatre gown. Redman was just finishing up his preoperative scrub and without looking up shouted, 'Availability, affability and ability, in that order! These are the hallmarks of success in surgery.'

These standards apply to the intern as much as they apply to the registrar trying to get on the scheme to train or the specialist trying to get a hospital post; if you're not there when people call, then who gives a damn how nice or how able you are. It especially applies to the process of getting referrals out in the big wide world, post-training. For general practitioners referring patients to a surgeon, their major concern is whether they are available to see the patient, who is often anxious and needs to be seen without delay. How nice they are to the patients and how competent they are as surgeons take second and third place.

In reality, general practitioners are often the worst judges of competence. Yet surgeons are at their behest, relying on their referral judgements. Recently, advertising has become more acceptable. There are now surgeons who rely on media advertising to influence patient decisions so that they in turn influence their family doctor to refer them. Some produce monthly newsletters. They will go to the extent of using their general practitioners as assistants in surgery, hence involving them more in the patient's care and, of course, in the fees.

'Availability, affability and ability. Remember these words and they'll stand you in good stead.'

John had always applied this aphorism to himself, and he became one of the most successful young surgical specialists in the hospital. Day or night, he was available for a general practitioner who needed to refer a patient. He never tired of accepting patients.

When John finally died of a massive coronary at the age of 40, he had one of the most successful practices in the hospital. Unfortunately, he left his wife with a quarter of a million dollars' worth of debts to service.

This night, however, there was no death in his eyes. He was in the hospital doing the thing he loved the most – operating. He had seen a 16-year-old girl with right iliac fossa pain in casualty that night, and decided she might have appendicitis. Lucy Morgani was a beautiful girl with shoulder-length hair that looked like golden silk thread. She had become ill during a party she had been to earlier in the evening. At first it was just nausea, and then came tell-tale right-sided abdominal pain. She was consented in casualty for the operation and then sent up to theatres. The anaesthetic registrar, Jan Nederthal, was in his first year of training. He rang the boss on call, who sleepily asked a few questions about what sounded like a routine case and said, 'Go ahead and call me if you have trouble.' It was a well-known phenomenon that a registrar's competence increased dramatically in the eyes of the boss between the hours of midnight and 6 am. The boss got to enjoy the hard-earned luxury of sleep and was unlikely to come in during those hours, so residents and registrars did more complex procedures than they might otherwise do.

Lucy had already had an intravenous cannula inserted and, after flushing it with normal saline, Jan injected some thiopentone and suxamethonium and prepared to ventilate her prior to intubation. These were the two medications that were used to put a person to sleep. Thiopentone induced sleep, while sux – as we lovingly called it – paralysed the muscles and made it easier to operate on the abdomen. The problem is it also paralyses the diaphragm, so a patient, once given sux, needs to be ventilated artificially.

Jan's knuckles were white as he held the mask in place. He had beads of sweat around his forehead. His assistant had not arrived yet; he had decided to proceed anyway as it was a simple case. John and I scrubbed at the bay in readiness.

'He's a bit green, isn't he?' said John, who was uncomfortable with the anaesthetist's lack of experience.

His hunch was right. The first sign of trouble was the sickening sound of suction tubing attempting to swallow solid material from the back of someone's throat. Lucy had just vomited up a large quantity of partially digested food. Most of this had entered her lungs, which were now being dissolved by the strong hydrochloric acid from the stomach.

'I thought you said she was fasted!' Jan glowered at John.

'That's what she said downstairs. Didn't you take the history?' John threw the blame straight back at the anaesthetic registrar. This was not a surgical call and everyone knew it. It was up to the anaesthetist to ensure that the patient was thoroughly screened prior to an operation. They are primarily responsible for the patient's life. The surgeon gets the glory while the anaesthetist keeps them alive. There was a standard joke defining anaesthesia that was often quoted: 'Anaesthesia is the half-awake keeping the half-asleep alive while the half-witted try to half-murder them.'

'She's hard to ventilate. Get the assistant here *stat*. Get McCormack in as well!' There was panic in Jan's voice and his face betrayed his fear. He knew, as did all in the theatre, that this girl was in big trouble.

Her oxygen saturation was dropping, despite being on 100 per cent concentrations. She was blue and getting worse. The monitors have blood-oxygen saturation reporting that is based on beeps of sound that drop in pitch as the oxygen saturation drops in concentration. The beeps were going through their choral fugue now. Soprano, changing to alto. A few more beeps and then they became a low tenor voice. The monitor read 70 per cent. At that level, the patient was in dangerous territory. After this came the slide into brain hypoxia, then brain damage. She was only a couple of minutes from a slippery slide to disaster.

'The sucker's blocked!'

In fact it was full and the nurse was changing the bags so it would continue to evacuate the vomit that now filled the back of Lucy's throat. Jan looked up. 'Quickly, for God's sake!' He was visibly shaking. 'Get help from ICU!' he shouted.

I unscrubbed and went to ring ICU. The senior registrar was down in the outer wards assessing a patient – he would be twenty minutes even if he ran. I relayed the unwelcome message. I could hear ectopic beats in the ECG. This was an ominous sign. The heart was straining because of the lack of oxygen. I rang McCormack, but his wife said he was on his way.

Lucy was now a rather deep shade of navy blue. Jan was attempting to intubate her with little success. He could not get a good view of the back of her throat, and her vocal cords were hidden by large chunks of fish fillet she had eaten earlier that evening, mixed with a significant amount of beer. He connected the tube to the hand ventilator and blew copious amounts of oxygen into her. Her upper abdomen increased dramatically in size. In his panic, Jan had placed the tube that was meant to offer Lucy's lungs life-saving oxygen into her gullet instead. This was a fatal mistake.

Jan took the tube out of the oesophagus and tried again to place it in the trachea. This time he succeeded. He put a sucker down the tube to clear large debris and started to ventilate her lungs. Her colour improved only marginally.

Dr McCormack finally arrived. He silently took over.

'What's the story?' he asked without looking at Jan.

'Um, she aspirated, I had trouble ventilating her . . . Um . . .' Jan was mumbling.

John and I looked at each other, each thanking God that it was not our necks on the chopping block. All of us knew that Jan Nederthal had not been equal to a task for which he had probably had enough training. No case can ever be taken for granted as routine. What we do to patients is dangerous, and some die as a result of our attempts to help them and not as a result of the disease they presented for.

We waited for an interminable time as McCormack ventilated Lucy by hand, improving her oxygen status.

'Her lungs feel like concrete. How much did she aspirate?' He looked at Nederthal with disdain.

'Quite a bit . . . I was told she was fasted . . . there was quite a bit . . .' He was stammering. His adrenaline levels were off the scale and he was not recovered from the events of the previous half hour. He had panicked. Anaesthetics was not a specialty that allowed for the luxury of panic. Jan knew that it was probably his panic that had contributed to what was almost certainly going to be Lucy's demise. She was OK for now, but the stomach acid would be doing damage to her lungs as they watched.

'Did you say you were TOLD? Did you assess her yourself?' McCormack was cherry-red in the face with anger.

'No, I asked her. She said she had not eaten or drunk anything since this morning.' Jan was defending the indefensible.

'Even so, why didn't you do a rapid sequence induction?'

Jan Nederthal should have conducted the anaesthetic with an assistant whose role it would have been to place pressure on the throat after the anaesthetic drugs had been injected to ensure that even if there was vomiting, that the oesophagus was obstructed and there would be no spillage into the lungs. Routines were there for a purpose. Jan had ignored a simple yet life-saving routine.

McCormack knew it was game, set and match. He looked at John and said, 'OK, get started and make it quick.'

I re-scrubbed and joined him at the operating table. He already had the incision made and was fishing inside with his index finger for the appendix. Out came a white, virginal appendix, with no sign of inflammation. He started to take it out as he was bound to do. The purse string went on, the tie was applied, the vessel controlled and the appendix removed. It was like poetry being read aloud.

Two days later, Lucy Morgani died in ICU from massive lung infections. It was made even more tragic by the fact that her pregnancy test had been positive the night of her admission.

Months of investigation, mortality and morbidity meetings and medical legal reports ensued. Eventually, her mother and stepfather received a large out-of-court settlement. By the time it was paid to them some three years later they had spent – on credit – large sums of money on cars, holidays and assorted orders from TV home shopping in the hope that this would all be covered by the payout.

It wasn't. Perhaps the spending was some way of reducing the pain of losing their daughter. But, of course, no amount of spending was going to bring back the girl they had lost. Sometimes, the compensation payout becomes the sole aim of aggrieved relatives. Is it that they see it as punishment for the doctor? Is it that they feel a sense of justice? We do not have our loved one, but the compensation paid for a holiday so that we could grieve properly.

Four months after Lucy's death, Jan Nederthal was found in his room with several ampoules' worth of potassium chloride in his system, which he'd injected. The potassium had stopped his heart. It was a quick and painless death that coincided with, but was not officially acknowledged as a result of, his expulsion from the anaesthetic scheme.

Jan was the fourth doctor of my contemporaries to commit suicide. It was a high death rate when one took our numbers into account. To some of us, our profession was all that we defined ourselves by. I was nothing without medicine. I was nothing without the title of Doctor. In some cases, when that is taken away from you, there is nothing left.

Perhaps without this hyper-association, one could not make it through the training program. I had heard of some doctors in my year who left medicine after their internship and entered a career in business or, more commonly, the pharmaceutical trade. I could not imagine anyone doing that. It was unfathomable. I was surgery, and surgery was me.

CHAPTER 7

A Punitive God

Earth is rocking in space!
And the thunders crash up with a roar upon roar,
And the eddying lightnings flash fire in my face,
And the whirlwinds are whirling the dust round and round –
And the blasts of the winds universal leap free
And blow each other upon each, with a passion of sound,
And æther goes mingling in storm with the sea!
Such a curse on my head, in a manifest dread,
From the hand of your Zeus has been hurtled along!
O my mother's fair glory! O Æther, enringing
All eyes with the sweet common light of thy bringing,
Dost see how I suffer this wrong?

'PROMETHEUS AMID HURRICANE AND EARTHQUAKE'
FROM *PROMETHEUS BOUND* BY AESCHYLUS

Being a surgical registrar at the Victoria Hospital was the closest thing to being God without being God. The consultants were God. Registrars ruled the life of the interns and residents and decided when we slept. They decided when we rested. Even as a third-year resident, if I were to have a good day, it would be by the grace of my registrar. Bad days were also decided for me by my registrar. I ate when they allowed me to eat. I could not wait to join their club and get onto the advanced surgical scheme.

Some residents could not hand over the locus of control and survived badly. They questioned, they struggled, and they became a nuisance to themselves, their patients and, most importantly, to their registrars. These juniors did not end up doing surgery.

I learned early on to be present for as long as it took to satisfy my registrar and make him or her happy. If they needed to abuse someone, I was there. If they needed to hate someone, I let them hate me.

Being Muslim made this easy. You learned to surrender to the will of God. Life, death, happiness, sadness, poverty, riches – all these were granted by the grace of God and had a purpose. The holy Koran says, 'Often you think something is bad for you and it turns out to be good.' So accept the will of God. The fact that, for the time being, God was on earth in the form of a surgical registrar was really a small leap of faith.

A name like Mohamed did not endear me to the keepers of surgical posts at the Victoria Hospital. While there was never any overt sign of outward discrimination, I was subtly made aware of my slightly lower rank in comparison to my colleagues.

When a colleague and I assisted at laparoscopic colectomies during my residency, we were asked about our backgrounds. Laparoscopy, or keyhole surgery, was a new technique and each operation would take much longer than its traditional, open equivalent. To resect a bowel (colectomy) using laparoscopy was an especially lengthy procedure and one had a lot of time for chat while slowly working through the various steps of the operation.

'Mohamed, where are you from?' I'd be asked.

'Well, I was born in Ghana, Africa. My parents are Lebanese and I was brought up a Muslim, hence the name.' I would recite the explanation that I knew they needed to hear. I always tried to reassure them with a concluding, 'But I am an Australian now.'

'Which school did you go to?'

This was always a killer. My parents were working-class people. I had been lucky to go to any school. I had gone to the local public high school and had the marks to study Medicine.

I became more immune to this line of questioning when I passed my surgical primary on my first attempt while others needed several attempts, and even more comfortable after I published several papers at an early stage of my career. By then there was no way to exclude me from the surgical scheme without appearing grossly discriminatory. Even so, there was considerable grumbling in the corridors about my appointment. I had beaten the blue-eyed favourites, the boys from private schools whose fathers were friends of the establishment. I developed a thick skin. I would make comments myself about being Lebanese, about having gone to an undesirable high school.

The need to constantly establish my credibility took its toll. It was depressing. However, it was not as depressing as the term I found myself doing that year: head and neck surgery.

Patients would often come in with ulcers that had festered in their mouths and necks for years as they'd slowly grown in size and smell. The insidious nature of these growths led the patient to ignore them, deny their horrific implications and hide them from the light of day. Eventually, the spouse could no longer ignore the smell, or they would go to a GP who actually examined them, or they themselves were concerned about the ooze onto their shirts or the fact that their dentures would no longer fit.

Inevitably, these cancers were smoking-related and the first thing the patients did when we told them the diagnosis and the cause was to stop smoking.

Each time this happened, the words of that Carole King song, 'It's too late, baby, now, it's too late,' came rushing into my mind. I would look at the patient and my mouth would encourage their cessation of this one vice while my heart was saying, 'For God's sake enjoy it while you can, because you are doomed.'

The mainstay of treatment for these cancers was surgery or radiotherapy. With radiotherapy the patient could maintain a semblance of normality of appearance. With surgical excision, their facial appearance was often altered. A cancer of the lower jaw might require the entire jaw to be removed and replaced, usually by bone and muscle from the forearm. Occasionally, artificial resins were used that were later clad with skin. The end result was functionally acceptable, but left a lot to be desired aesthetically.

There was a quiet abhorrence in my heart about what we were doing to these patients. At no time was a patient offered the alternative: a quiet and peaceful death. Euthanasia.

The basic assumption was that life was to be clung to at every cost. This basic assumption – to my never-ending surprise – was shared by all the patients. Or so it seemed. I wondered what I would do in the same situation. Depending on the extent of disfigurement, I was sure I would opt for death rather than a life of ugliness. I surrounded myself with beauty, with music, with art. I could not live with a face that would disgust me each morning. *Narcissus liveth*. And why not?

The surgery itself was challenging. The only thing that made the term bearable was working with Dr Pondenstein. He was precise and didactic, and his dissections were like watching the pages of a textbook come to life. He was incredibly focused on his work. He was also unusually reticent about engaging in any conversation that was not case-related and, even then, these exchanges were abrupt and pointed.

During operations there is often friendly and innocuous banter among the staff. Not with Pondenstein. I'd often spend sixteen hours in theatre without a word being exchanged.

Sometimes he would sigh. A deep, long, painful sigh. I had heard a similar sigh from men whose life had just expired. I would occasionally wait in the room of one of my patients whom I knew was close to death to see that transition between life and no life. Such a definite change from a patient to meat, from body to carcass. Always, the sigh. Perhaps it was the soul leaving the body, dragging with it some memento of life's breath. The absolute stillness of the eyes. The cold blotchiness of the skin.

Pondenstein gave me the impression that my fresh optimism and ambition in surgery was slightly bemusing to him. Each day, we'd do wards rounds together and I'd try to engage him in conversation about a myriad of topics that I felt might be of interest to him. It became a challenge to find a field of discussion about which Pondenstein would say more than a handful of polite words before dismissing it. For six months he said little more to me than was absolutely necessary, and my quest failed miserably.

Still, I made sure I looked after his patients with absolute dedication. Often I would stay overnight in the hospital with a patient just to make sure the skin flap that had been constructed to cover some major dissection was viable, and that no one inexperienced tampered with it. I was always there before he arrived. I stayed later than he did. I was at his side constantly doing his bidding. I gave my life's blood to that term. Perhaps I was, in fact, compensating for my own internal turmoil about the whole issue of giving heroic medical care to patients who, in my view, would be better off dead. Who makes that decision? Who governs it?

Eventually the day came when my term was over. Pondenstein's duty was to provide me with feedback about my performance. We did our final ward round and he stopped in the corridor. There was the sigh; a long period of silence.

'I suppose I should give you some feedback or something,' he said slowly.

I waited in silence.

'I know you think you are different and need to impress, but my advice is don't try so hard.'

With that, he walked away. The intern who had been on the ward round grinned in an embarrassed way. I tried to smile the broad, beaming smile that I had perfected throughout my life. I used it to hide all emotion. But it would not come easily today. Instead, I succeeded in contorting my face so that it looked like the patients we had operated on that term. It was a long while before I could once again look in the mirror and see normality.

I was transferred shortly afterwards to colorectal surgery. The team I was assigned to was to give a surgical grand rounds presentation. Another surgeon – Dr Pears – asked me if I could help him with it. This normally implied I would do the work of chasing references and making slides. On this occasion he meant, 'You do it, son, and I will be there in the audience.' We had a patient with a rare tumour of the small intestine that I thought would make a good presentation, both from a diagnostic and a therapeutic point of view.

I decided to go a step further and review all the cases of this condition in the hospital and present them as a research project with recommendations. This was almost unheard of for a second-year resident. It took me several weekends and evenings to gather all the records from 1945 onwards. I categorised them, drew conclusions, looked up the litera-ture and made slides. Finally, the day arrived. I was ready; I knew more about melanoma of the small intestine than anyone. I had polished my presentation to the point of knowing it by heart. This was unprecedented for surgical grand rounds, which was usually a casual affair with a few hand-drawn overheads.

I was introduced. I then stepped to the podium and commenced the show. What a show! My presentation was good. It was better than any of the speakers that year. The Department of Surgery had never before been treated to anything like this. A lot of interest was generated and several questions were asked at the end of my talk.

Dr Levi, the head of the department, asked if all of the patients I had reviewed were Dr Pear's patients. I replied that I reviewed all the patients with melanoma of the small intestine who had presented to the hospital, regardless of their treating medical officer. After a few other questions I sat back in my seat. Several members of the department looked over to where I sat and grinned, sniggering to themselves. As soon as the meeting ended, Dr Levi came over to me. I stood ready to receive his congratulations on my presentation. I held out my hand in anticipation.

He looked at it, and then at the top of his voice – so that every member of the department could hear – said, 'If you ever use one of my patients again in a study and you do not consult me then I will make sure you never work in surgery. Is that clear?'

I was dumbfounded. I hesitated.

'IS THAT CLEAR?'

'Yes . . . sir.'

Apart from 'yes sir' or 'no sir', there was no wisdom in saying anything in self-defence. He was the boss. The advice from Arthur Miller's *Death of a Salesman* came rushing back to me: 'Son, you've got to work hard, play hard and smile hard.' Well, I did at least two of those things. I never played.

*

The time came to submit my application for an accredited training job in surgery. The chances of getting this were slim. There were almost 120 doctors with their basic surgical training complete and only one job on the training scheme that year. In my favour were the degrees I had obtained part-time while doing my basic training, the research papers and the prizes for research that I had gained. Against me was the intense competition from my fellow residents who were talented, had played the game equally, had done the hours, and had kept their records clean. It was unfair that any of us should miss out, but the positions were rationed and many residents didn't achieve their dreams. In later years I would meet them socially and that sense of loss seemed to survive the aeons. 'I never made it,' was not a thought I wanted to live with for the rest of my life.

I needed time to think about my future in surgery and, specifically, which particular branch I was to sub-specialise in. I had, by now, done a term of at least three months in all the main branches and subspecialties. My wife was on rotation at a country hospital and I didn't feel like being on my own so I moved back to my parents' house. This afforded me thinking time without interruption for the menial tasks of life. My clothes were washed, my food was cooked and I was left alone at night.

Night-time was thinking time. The quiet, black blanket of inactivity which is draped upon the world removes distraction and focuses the mind. Combine this with loud music played through headphones and you can create a surreal landscape out of the most common rooms. I'd lie on my bed with the 'Chopin E minor' piano concerto streaming into my brain through the east and west city gates.

Did I really want to continue in surgery or, for that matter, in medicine generally? I had not found happiness so far. Surely this was only because I was still training. The specialists had carefree existences: they were rich, they drove fast cars, they lived in big houses. Only one thing divided me from them: getting onto the accredited training scheme and then, at the end of the four-year training program, the Fellowship examination of the College of Surgeons. The whole experience was really a test of stamina, knowledge, character and mettle rivalled only by the meanest feats of human endeavour.

Here was climbing Everest, winning Olympic gold in the marathon and joining the French Foreign Legion all rolled into one.

I had yet to decide in which subspecialty to become a registrar. Cardiac surgery was glamorous but repetitive. One did the same operation every day, several times a day. Neurosurgery was exacting and challenging. But patients mostly became vegetables, alive and yet dead. And they were the successes – the others died. Colorectal was smelly; upper gastro-intestinal surgery was too busy after hours and the patients were very sick. Plastic surgery was too superficial.

That left urology: kidneys, bladders, prostates, impotence, stones, incontinence. Not very glamorous but it paid well, had a friendly training program, and when you were on call you were hardly ever called out.

And so it was decided. I wondered what it would be like telling people about my decision to do urology. I started with my parents.

'I have decided to do urology,' I said at breakfast the next day.

My father had a proud look in his eyes. 'Neurology is very good. I have always wanted you to do nerves. My son the brain surgeon.'

'No, I mean urology – wee wees, prostates, bladders, penises.'

Stunned silence.

My mother this time. 'Why would you want to specialise in this field? What is in it for you? What will our friends say?'

'Trust me, it's a good field.'

'You know best . . . but . . .'

Obviously it was not going to be an easy task. This was not a field with which you made easy conversation at parties. *Hi, I am a urologist. Why do I like it? Well, to tell you the truth, you actually do some good for humanity and very few patients die. I do not like death. I do not enjoy the dance with the Angel. I like doing operations. This is the ideal compromise. Can you understand?*

'Well, that is really interesting . . . Oh, there's Brad . . . Hi Brad – excuse me.'

But somebody has to look after sick dicks, for God's sake. The interviews for the training scheme were held later that month. The panel saw fit to offer me a job. I was now a God, a registrar. I had power over interns and residents. I ruled the roost.

My next two years would be spent in general surgery as a surgical registrar, and my final three doing urology as a senior registrar. My path was determined; now I simply had to survive it.

CHAPTER 8
The Avoidance Game

Under the wide and starry sky,
Dig the grave and let me lie.
Glad did I live and gladly die,
And I laid me down with a will.
This be the verse you grave for me:
Here he lies where he longed to be;
Home is the sailor, home from the sea,
And the hunter home from the hill.

'REQUIEM' BY ROBERT LOUIS STEVENSON

Training in any surgical specialty is rigorous and it was only tolerable if you considered it a gigantic game with several sub-games. After theatre you played the evening avoidance game – you made sure the patients did not die overnight while trying to get home as early as possible so that you could have a life of your own before the next game began. A life of your own was really a euphemism for sleep. You were lucky to get home by 9 pm. Most of my colleagues had married by now, or were planning to get married. The married ones constantly complained about the expectations of their spouses. I was lucky to have married very early and, more importantly, to have married a doctor. She understood all too well. In fact, it was not infrequent for her to be home later than me. We would then go out for dinner somewhere local and crawl into bed late at night. Then the next day started again.

The morning avoidance game was the tightest; it was a constant challenge to play this one effectively. The rules were simple: you had to see as many of your ward patients as possible and get to theatre on time by 8 am, so that the boss was not kept waiting. The secret of this game was to spend only enough time with each patient to ensure that they were still alive when you got out of theatre that afternoon, often after 7 pm.

In an average surgical service you would have thirty patients under your care. Some had been operated on, others were waiting to be operated on. Nursing handover was at 7 am. You did not dare disturb this process. If you wanted to be accompanied by a nurse during your ward round, the earliest you could start was 7.30 am. Hence, half an hour was allowed every morning for the morning avoidance game.

'Good morning, Mr Smith. How are you today?' The man looks well from this end of the bed.

'Doctor, I'm so glad you're here. I've had a terrible night. I was in so much pain, I couldn't sleep a wink.'

'That's no good – let's see what you are charted for pain.'

I look at the chart. His temperature is fine, his vital signs are strong. There are no gradients. I lose interest. I need to get to the next patient. 'Could we get a pain consult for this gentleman, please?' I say, addressing no one in particular, yet the assembled crowd around me, consisting of the interns, residents and the charge, automatically divide the tasks and orders among themselves according to job description.

A pain-team consultation may take days to arrive. The intern will call the pain registrar later that morning when he gets around to this task. She will answer with a frantic tone; she is busy and hassled. The intern will tell her about the patient. She will give the usual response.

'I'll get to it when I can. Patient's name? Ward? OK, bye.'

The intern ticks his list. The patient's name is now off the intern's list and on her list. The job of pain registrar is a busy one. It may be the next day or even later that week before she gets to Mr Smith.

'Doctor, I need to know what's going to happen to me? I'm so worried about this cancer. What will happen to my family?'

Emotionally laden material – this requires more time than the allotted one minute I have with this patient. Do I spend this time or do I avoid?

'Mr Smith, it is only natural to be worried. I will arrange for someone to come and speak to you about your feelings and anxieties.'

Morning avoidance game played to perfection.

'Sister, could we please get the social worker to see Mr Smith,' I say as I walk to the next patient.

This one is sick. Vital signs have been sagging overnight. The patient has had three infusions – a bad sign. There is an inverse proportion between survival and the number of infusions – in fact, tubes – a patient is connected to. This, of course, is totally unscientific and unproven, yet holds true.

'Can we get the renal team to assess this patient? We also need the cardiologists. Get them urgently.' This avoids the need to spend my time assessing this patient. Getting a consult diverts the blame away. Physicians have time to listen to the chest, to look at each blood result and consider its true cosmic meaning while jiggling infusions with the deft subtleness of an illusionist. Surgeons do; physicians think.

I need to get to theatre.

The boss is already there; the time is 8.05 am. The morning avoidance game has not been played well enough.

'I'm sorry I am late. We have some sickies up on the ward.'

'Good afternoon, Doctor Khadra, nice of you to join us.'

Struck out again. My assessment as a surgeon was not only about how well I operated, but was also about time and people management. A patient complaint could end your career. Being perpetually late for theatre could end your career. Balance and skill was developed the hard way. I taught myself, as all surgeons do. There were no time-management or people-management skills training offered to surgeons. You learned or you got out.

Each day was filled with operating. At centre stage in the surgical theatre was the diva, the boss, He Upon Whom Your

Life Depended. A bad report from one of the many bosses for whom you worked during your training could potentially end your career. There was no natural justice to this system. It was a system that weeded out undesirable surgeons. Undesirable was, of course, a subjective assessment.

As a surgical registrar, when you were not actually working, you were trying to study for the Fellowship examination. This was the final barrier examination set in surgery. It came around faster than any trainee ever predicted. Anatomy, physiology, pathology; poring over the many tomes that described your specialty. Many of my textbooks had large stains in them from where I had fallen asleep reading them and had drooled saliva mixed with coffee into the pages. The spirit was willing to study and pass the examination but the flesh was weak.

Every third night I worked an overnight shift, which meant starting at 7 am and finishing the next night at 7 or 8 pm. Every third week I was on for the weekend, which meant I commenced work at 7 am on Saturday morning and worked through until Monday night.

There was a definite pattern to these shifts. Saturday morning was busy with handover from the teams that had been on overnight. Then came the multitude of consultant ward rounds you were expected to go on. These were mostly social calls so patients would not complain that they had not seen the boss and hence resist paying the bill, especially if they were privately insured. No work was done on these rounds. You had to mop up after each of them and see the patients again to perform simple tasks like writing up their fluid orders, examining their chest, making certain that no calf thrombosis was present and ensuring that they would get out of the hospital alive.

Saturday afternoon was quiet – usually. One could retire to the quarters and watch TV and wait for the sporting traumas, which would start to trickle into casualty at about 4 pm. Then there would be the renal colic in the early evening and, finally, at about 11 pm, the alcohol-induced road trauma. Young men mostly, who had recently learned to drive and felt that driving at a speed below the capabilities of their souped-up cars was akin to sacrilege. To add to the challenge, they dulled their senses with ethanol and distracted their attentions with the convivial company of friends who were willing to lay down their lives in passenger seats.

The ambulance drivers had the worst job. They had to cope with straightening out bits of bodies that were bent in the most origami-like fashion. When the injured arrived in my casualty department, they had fluid running, they had splints and were usually, but not always, alive. I was not responsible for coaxing them into surviving the next few days. I only had to keep them alive until the team on call took over, and the sooner the better, but this could take hours or days.

In the meantime, patients would have to pack up their emotional needs and take them up with the next shift. Head traumas, spinal and orthopedic injuries, chest and abdominal trauma were all likely, and one had to exclude and treat each of these individually. It was messy, unsatisfying work. One was always filled with anger about the pointlessness of saving the morons, the ones who had drugged or drunk themselves to oblivion and then decided to get behind the wheel of a car. It was made especially tragic when they took innocent bystanders in other cars or on pedestrian walkways with them into the land of injury or, in the worst of all cases, death. The economic drain was enormous. The most severely injured trauma victims were in hospital and then rehabilitation for up to three months. The cost per patient would run into millions of dollars.

By the early hours of Saturday morning, the surgical registrar was in the theatre with the trauma or an appendix or whatever had come in during the evening. When I finally came out of the theatre it was often dawn on Sunday. The same performance was repeated again but without the boss's ward rounds. By Monday morning, the combination of sleep deprivation, ugly encounters and the overwhelming sight of torn human flesh made one manic. You fronted up to the morning ward round looking haggard and woebegone and yet somehow you felt fresh, on top of the world. Your judgement, however, was not fresh. Your skills were not fresh. By Monday night the manic phase had worn away and there was a deep, weary depression. You went home, slept, and by Tuesday morning you were back into action.

The only saving grace was that, for the most part, medicine is really a game of reflexes and mindless pattern recognition, and the theatre is often a refuge from common sense. After a while, you can go into automatic and survive despite the worst intellectual impediments. Surgeons push on despite lack of sleep, through the emotional destruction of divorces and the death of loved ones.

I decided to take a year off my training before proceeding to the next year and complete the research for my PhD. I would become an expert on one of the nerves to the bladder and would know more about it than anyone else in the world. Know lots about very little. That is called specialising.

CHAPTER 9

Stabat Mater

Stabat Mater dolorosa
iuxta Crucem lacrimosa,
dum pendebat Filius.

Cuius animam gementem,
contristatam et dolentem
pertransivit gladius.

O quam tristis et afflicta
fuit illa benedicta,
mater Unigeniti!

THIRTEENTH-CENTURY HYMN

At the Cross her station keeping,
Stood the mournful Mother weeping,
Close to her Son to the last.

Through her heart, His sorrow sharing,
All His bitter anguish bearing,
Now at length the sword has passed.

With what pain and desolation,
With what noble resignation,
The Mother watched her dying Son.

Doing research was a wonderful way to take a break from surgical training. It entailed reading in the library, coming up with a hypothesis and then conducting experiments meant to prove a hypothesis right or wrong.

To survive financially, I had to do on-call night shifts. These brought me in contact with a large variety of patients from other services, medical and surgical. Of course, I had no direct responsibilities for them apart from ensuring they were cared for overnight – their teams took over in the morning – but it gave me a great opportunity to see another aspect of healthcare.

Mrs Deeb was a devoutly religious woman. She looked out over the hospital car park with deeply hollowed eyes and the edges of her slit-like mouth downturned. Both these features adorned a wrinkled face framed by a floral pattern of polyester hibiscuses that made up the hijab – the head covering she wore that she constantly adjusted to ensure her hair was hidden from any men other than her closest relatives. Her Koran was never far from her. She wore a grey coat over her olive-green dress that she had bought for a bargain during her last trip to Lebanon.

That had been an eventful trip. It started so happily. She had saved up for over eight years from the meagre widow's benefits she had been granted after her husband's death from lung cancer. Out of these benefits, she had managed to bring up Ahmad and Lamees, her two children.

Her brother Fawzi had migrated at about the same time and he and his family looked after her well and made sure she had the basics of life. He played father to the two children, who were eight and ten when their own father died.

Her trip to Lebanon had turned into a nightmare when Ahmad had a nosebleed that would not stop. They had tried everything from packing ground coffee beans up his nostrils to pressure and ice. Nothing worked. Eventually, when he was feeling faint from blood loss, they put him in the back of her cousin's station wagon and drove at high speed from Tyre in the south of Lebanon to the hospital in Beirut. There, cash had to be handed over in advance of any treatment.

With her son bleeding to death, she had no option but to run down with her cousin to the jewellery store in Hamra Street and trade in her wedding bangle, ring and necklace for immediate cash (obviously at a huge discount). Every blood test, every transfusion, every examination, every consultation, every treatment racked up the already extensive bill. She had not been able to afford travel insurance but now was paying for it many times over.

Her uncle Jawad came to the rescue and settled the balance of the hospital stay as long as she got onto the next plane with her son and daughter and departed Lebanon. She was picked up at the airport as soon as she arrived back in the country and was taken straight to the Victoria Hospital. Thank God for free medical care, she thought.

Her daughter, Lamees, was now the woman of the house. She was forced to leave her studies in the final year of high school. The school made some enquiries and sent a social worker or two, but fundamentally there was no choice and Lamees had to grow up quickly. Mrs Deeb had high hopes for her. A tear ran down her cheek as she remembered the regrets she felt about Lamees' abandoned education.

Then there was Ahmad. In Lebanon, they had told her he had the flu and would recover soon. In the hospital here, they were experts at not hiding the truth. She now knew her son had leukaemia that had invaded his brain.

The chemotherapy that Ahmad was being treated with did not seem to be getting into the brain. Mrs Deeb was told a tube needed to be inserted into his spinal fluid to allow the chemotherapy direct access into the fluid surrounding his brain. She was told this would be uncomfortable for Ahmad. This was a gross understatement.

A junior medical officer came around the next day. Sasha Cumberland was a gorgeous blonde who was desired by every male in the hospital. She did not believe in white coats; she felt they created a barrier between her and her patients. She was wearing a Chanel singlet, white with flowered sequins, and Armani jeans. Her high-heeled sandals meant she was heard long before she came into a room. Sasha was cautioned by the senior staff nurse because of the disturbance it caused on night duty – 'Patients have complained; it isn't professional; there is a dignity about being a doctor.'

Sasha told her to 'fuck off'.

'Hello. I'm Sasha Cumberland. I'm here to put an intrathecal catheter into Ahmad.' Of course, Mrs Deeb did not understand a word that Sasha said, and for that matter the reverse was true. Two cultures, two outlooks, two faiths now squared off at each other.

Mrs Deeb despised Sasha from the start. She looked at this girl and thought even the whores who stood outside the nightclubs of the Hamra district in Beirut were better dressed than she was. She looked at Sasha's ill-kept hair, the sides of her breasts that her singlet revealed and could not believe the disrespect to dying patients and to the holy profession that this girl represented.

To Sasha, Mrs Deeb was irrelevant. She had been scrutinised and judged by better people than this. She felt sorry for the migrant peasant who could allow polyester to adorn her skin. She could smell her armpits from the end of the bed and her cheap shoes were something else altogether. No words were spoken but both knew the other's mind.

When Sasha reached up to hang saline on a stand, Mrs Deeb could see her umbilical stud, which further irritated her. She said nothing. This girl, who claimed to be a doctor, was here to help Ahmad. Whatever she looked like, as long as she was able to give him some relief from the pain, to help him get better, that was all that mattered.

Sasha had asked Ahmad to get on his side and curl up in a ball. She washed her hands, but then took a phone call. It was Joe Carlos asking her out on a date. Mrs Deeb did not understand the conversation in English and nor had she understood what Sasha was planning to do. She stood up to comfort Ahmad, who by now was feeling immensely uncomfortable on his side. His bedsores were savage and any movement caused him pain.

Sasha washed her hands again, apologised and set up her tray. She took the cool alcohol wipe, painted it liberally over Ahmad's back and when his back flinched and arched she said, 'A bit cold, mate?'

Ahmad nodded.

Sasha took the needle off the tray and without warning stuck it into the small of Ahmad's back. He flinched again. 'Stay still now,' said Sasha in that high-pitched monotonous tone that professionals use. Inherent in this utterance is that all is OK and I am doing a good job, and you are ungrateful.

It took half an hour of jabbing and moving the needle around to get in between the vertebral columns at the correct angle so that the needle could approach the spinal cord and penetrate the dura, the tough outer lining within which was held the nerves and the spinal fluid. Sasha knew what to do; it was just that she had never done it before. Mrs Deeb and Ahmad, of course, did not know any of that.

Eventually, the catheter was in and clear fluid dripped out. Sasha collected some into tubes and then capped the catheter for the chemotherapy sisters to come the next day and place their potions.

That afternoon, Ahmad had been unable to empty his bladder. I was called to place another catheter, this one into his bladder. He was a sad young man who had endured much in his short years. His mother was grateful to speak in Arabic to me and I comforted her as best I could.

That week I was doing a whole run of evenings and I would try and call up to see Mrs Deeb before my shift came to an end at midnight. Her favourite place to sit was at the window, overlooking the car park. It gave her some respite from the suffering in her son's room to see the comings and goings of the staff.

After three weeks the chemotherapy still had no effect. Now, Ahmad was lapsing in and out of consciousness. When he was conscious he screamed out in pain. His head would have most likely felt as if it was going to blow up. Sadly, that was exactly what was happening. The leukaemia cells were multiplying in his brain and causing the pressure to rise.

Within days the screams were such that he had to be moved to a private room normally reserved for VIPs – none of the patients in the five other beds surrounding him could sleep through his screams and Mrs Deeb fussing over him all night. She was constantly by his bedside. Once every couple of days, Lamees would come in and look after Ahmad while Mrs Deeb went home and had a wash and changed her clothes.

It was midnight and she could see the last of the evening shift leaving the hospital. One by one, nurses and orderlies would walk out into the darkness five floors down and then get into their cars. Mrs Deeb could recognise many of them. They had all, at one stage or other, looked after her son. Her poor son.

He was grunting tonight, neighing with pain. She had gone out to ask the nurses for some pain relief for him at 11 pm. That was shift changeover. There was handover, there was coffee to be drunk to get you started on the night shift, there was the usual spate of blood pressures and eventually, at 1.30 am, a nurse came around with an injection. Ahmad did not even flinch these days when he got injections. But Mrs Deeb still did. With every injection she felt as though her own skin was being pierced. Every discomfort was her discomfort.

She asked for the Lebanese doctor to be called.

'Dr Khadra. I am sorry to disturb you but Mrs Deeb is asking for you,' said the nurse on the end of the phone.

'But I am not looking after him,' I said. I paused. I could not say no. 'I will be down in an hour.'

It was 2 am now and Ahmad was still in pain, writhing now with an almost unconscious rhythm, each move accompanied with a grunt. Mrs Deeb turned away from the window and held his head under her left arm, kissing his forehead. 'Shush, shush, my darling, God give you peace. Shush, shush, my darling, God give you rest,' she whispered to him. 'Oh God, oh God, oh God,' she whispered, over and over to him.

'What is going to happen with him, Doctor?' She was speaking in Arabic and pleading with me to find a solution to her son's predicament.

I just held her hand. What could I say to help her pain, let alone her son's?

She got up again to wipe his brow. Ahmad settled for a while. Mrs Deeb wiped the tears from her eyes. His life was intolerable.

I stayed with her for a while. She settled back at the window and opened her Koran at the 36th chapter. A chapter that said to give comfort to the unfortunate and the dead. She looked at Ahmad. A thought suddenly struck her. There was no more hope.

She had read between the lines and understood the doctor clearly yesterday. The tone of his voice and the sadness in his face conveyed to her the message that they had reached the end of the line. How long was it going to be? She sobbed and tears ran away from her again. This poor boy of hers, was it not enough for him to grow up fatherless, having seen his father die, coughing blood and choking on his own spit. He had never done the many things that she had hoped he would do when he became a man. He wanted to be a doctor. He loved watching TV, but now the strobing set off epileptic seizures and he could no longer look at the screen. She thought to herself that he had never slept with a woman. She felt embarrassed to have thought it, but it was true.

Ahmad started grunting again. She had one page to go to finish the Surat Ya-Seen, the Sura of the dead.

'God's word is always truth.' She finished with the usual supplication and then kissed the spine of the book in respect. Put the Koran down. Ahmad was screaming now. The nurse came in.

'He has to be quiet, other patients are trying to sleep,' she said angrily to Mrs Deeb. 'Ahmad, please try and be quieter, I will bring you another injection, OK?' The nurse left. Ahmad continued to scream.

The nurse came back about 30 minutes later with a kidney dish containing an injection of morphine. She wiped his thigh with alcohol and plunged the needle deep into the muscle.

'It will work soon,' she said.

Mrs Deeb waited for her to leave. Enough was enough. She read the opening prayer of the Koran to herself, whispered in Ahmad's right ear, 'There is no God but one God and Mohammad is his prophet.' She then whispered the same in his left ear, 'There is no God but one God and Mohammad is his prophet.'

She looked at her dear son and could see him at his birth, she could see him in the backyard cutting his knee, she remembered him at his father's funeral where he had read out the prayer and brought everyone to tears. She remembered the start of this nightmare, the nosebleed that began so innocuously only months ago.

Mrs Deeb reached out her hand and cradled Ahmad's head; she gave him a long kiss on his forehead and uttered to herself, 'May God have mercy on your soul.'

She then placed his head in her chest and cradled it, pressing his face to her bosoms with the most profound love a mother could have. She squeezed his body to hers as if to pray, please let me be sick instead of my boy. Ahmad was by now too weak to struggle. He did not even try to push her away. Her hug had stopped him breathing. During the minute that she held him, his heart had stopped. Ahmad was dead.

She sat back at the window. Read another chapter of the Koran, chapter 37: the Merciful One. The time was now

5 am. She thought to herself, I am glad he is comfortable now.

A nurse came in to do observations of pulse and blood pressure. She could not feel a pulse. She felt for the carotid pulse but could not feel that either. She reached mindlessly for the bright red button on the wall and a cardiac arrest was called. Within seconds a number of doctors and nurses and orderlies arrived. When I walked back in, there was hardly room for me to stand. The nurse had already started heart massage. Soon another nurse put a mask on Ahmad's face and started to push oxygen into his lungs. Spit and sputum was making the mask very difficult to apply but she tried her best. The medical registrar waltzed in. He placed his hand on the neck – it was cold to touch. He took his torch and shone it into Ahmad's glazed eyes.

Mrs Deeb was staring out of the window. She had not engaged in any of the events that had occurred in the room. She was silently reading and reciting prayers and was used to doctors rushing in and out of the room.

'Fixed dilated pupils, bilaterally,' he shouted. 'When was he discovered?'

'Just now,' said the nurse. 'I called the alarm as soon as I found him.'

'He's gone. He's dead. Who are you?' The registrar looked at Mrs Deeb.

'This is his mother,' the nurse replied. 'She doesn't speak English.'

'Jesus Christ! Can someone get an interpreter?' he shouted.

CHAPTER 10

Justice Connolly

O for a draught of vintage, that hath been
Cooled a long age in the deep-delved earth,
Tasting of Flora and the country green,
Dance, and Provencal song, and sun-burnt mirth!
O for a beaker full of the warm South,
Full of the true, the blushful Hippocrene,
With beaded bubbles winking at the brim,
And purple-stained mouth;
That I might drink, and leave the world unseen,
And with thee fade away into the forest dim.

'ODE TO A NIGHTINGALE' BY JOHN KEATS

During my research year, I contemplated again what branch of surgery to go into. I had settled on urology but the thought of becoming a transplant surgeon kept rolling around in my head. I decided to give it a go, and if it was to be a fair go I needed to attach myself to the best transplant surgeon in the country, who happened to be Professor Ryan Schumacher.

Each week, during my research year, we would run into each other in the corridor leading to the Department of Surgery.

'Hello, Ahmet,' he would say. 'What are you up to?'

'It's Mohamed, sir. I am doing a PhD,' I would reply.

'A PhD. My, my. A PhD,' he would say as he strolled away.

The next week and every week, I had a similar conversation with him.

'Hello, Moustapha. What are you up to?'

'It is Mohamed. A PhD,' I would reply, with increasing exasperation.

'A PhD. My, my.'

Each time I met him, he would be gone before I had a chance to ask whether he would support me on the transplant scheme or not, so I decided to wait for an opportunity to assist him with a transplant. That opportunity presented itself almost immediately.

Right from the start, there was a problem with Justice Connolly. He stank of stale alcohol. He was in the anteroom to the theatre where fifteen doctors, nurses, technicians, orderlies, registrars and students were standing by to replace his alcohol-sizzled cirrhotic liver with a new one. Booze had brought him to this place and now he had a chance at a new life by being given a new liver. He had a chance to live again, to regain his colour, his manhood. Yet he was drunk.

Despite the massive cost to taxpayers for his liver transplant, despite the warnings, the repeated counselling, the various clinics, Justice Connolly continued to drink. He of course denied it every time he saw his doctor, and when the social workers called in to see him at home he was always out.

In the theatre, the surgeon, Professor Ryan Schumacher, and the anaesthetist, Dr Evangelica Sanchez, were caught in a bitter life-and-death struggle.

'I don't care who he is, transplanting this man while he continues to drink is tantamount to negligence.' Dr Sanchez was taking the moral high ground.

'I know, Evangelica, I know what you're saying, but be reasonable – he's one of the most prominent judges in this country. Not doing him now, having already harvested and when we're set to go is a complete waste of resources. We might as well flush the fucking liver down the gurgler.'

'Yeah, but he's drunk and you know what that means. He'll be back here next year with liver failure. Give the liver to someone who deserves it.' She was making her point emphatically.

Schumacher was silent because he knew they would go ahead anyway. He had the final say. No one dared to obstruct the great Schumacher.

'Harvesting' is the euphemism for taking another person's organs. The donor is usually – though not always – an unrecoverable head injury, but with functioning organs. In this case, the donor was an 18-year-old high-school student in rural Australia who had gone for a joy-ride on the back of his best friend's motorbike. Travelling down a dirt road just outside Wagga Wagga, they struck a pothole.

The driver got away with a broken femur, chest contusions and a pair of fractured forearms to boot. His friend's brain was mashed beyond repair. He had landed with such a thud that he severed several blood vessels suspended between his brain and his skull. They in turn bled and caused raised intracranial pressure. By the time he got to hospital, he had dilated pupils and global brain damage.

Though his brain was dead, his heart, lungs, kidneys and liver continued to function. They would function as long as his heart pumped blood into them and his lungs oxygenated that blood and got rid of the carbon dioxide. Brain death was a diagnosis made after testing the neurological function with an electroencephalograph and various clinical tests that defined the condition. He had tested positive straight across the board.

To see him in the ICU bed was to think that he was a normal, good-looking 18-year-old with his whole life in front of him. The monitor showed a good, strong heartbeat. The respirator pumped his chest up and down. However, he was dead.

Some religions define death as the departure of the soul from the body. Modern science, for the most part, has discounted the presence of a soul and goes by brain function. This represents the triumph of brain over heart, logic over emotion; empirical trumps the theoretical.

Once the diagnosis of brain death is made, the patient becomes a transplant donor if they have indicated their willingness prior to death, or if the next of kin give permission. In this case, the parents felt that at least some good could come of their only son's death.

From that point on, the patient is a living storage unit for organs – vital organs that give life to others who have functioning brains but non-functioning organs. The cornea, the lungs, the heart, the kidneys, the liver and many other parts can be reused. Recently the intestines, the pancreas and even the face have been transplanted. Up to ten recipients can benefit from one patient's death.

In most countries buying organs is illegal. They must be freely given. However, such is the nature of humanity that there are many countries where organs are sold on the open market. Poor families sell their kidneys and their blood in India. In China, executed prisoners are organ donors. In some parts of the world, people are kidnapped and used as organ donors.

In Western countries, the patient's blood type is broadcast to all transplant units and the best match is found for each of the patient's organs. We then harvest these organs. I was on call for transplant when the word came from Wagga Wagga. A private jet was chartered and a team of two surgeons, an anaesthetist and scrub nurse, went to retrieve the organs.

Even when you are used to it, organ harvesting is a difficult, emotional procedure. The incision is neck to pubis. The entire torso is flayed open. The first to be taken are the kidneys, then the liver, and, finally and quickly, the heart and lungs. The anaesthetic monitors are turned off at this point and there is total silence in the theatre as the patient is left as an empty, dead shell. The incision is closed with running sutures and the family take the body for burial or cremation.

The organs are put on ice and go to various parts of the country where others anxiously waiting for an organ, or death, get a second chance, a reprieve.

Justice Connolly was matched well for this liver. His own liver had been destroyed by years of filtering whisky on the rocks. Black Label was his favourite, but he would settle for anything from vodka to brandy.

'Well, if you want to go ahead, let's do it, but I want it recorded that I disagree.'

This was a cop-out and Dr Sanchez knew it. What was the point of throwing out the liver? It was too late to find someone else so she might as well give her consent to the operation. The alternative was certain death for the Justice. This would hit the papers immediately: 'Doctors refuse transplant for lawyer', 'Lawyer dies due to medico refusal to treat'.

The operation proceeded. The anaesthetic had commenced while the organs were on their way. Arterial lines in the wrist, central venous lines through the neck, two large fluid infusion lines in the arms and, of course, tracheal intubation. The surgeon then prepped and draped. A large inverted V-shaped incision was made in the upper abdomen just under the ribcage from the furthest extreme of the left side to the right side. Bed to bed is the best way to describe it.

Next came the laborious and dangerous task of taking the native liver out. It is not uncommon to need over 10 litres of blood for this phase of the operation. At some stage during this process, and hopefully before the liver is removed, the donor liver arrives. The esky it arrives in always reminds me of picnics.

I had been up now for over 24 hours from when the call first came through that there was a liver donor. The private jet that carried the liver landed just as the veins leading from the liver had been clamped in Justice Connolly. Several ambulances were waiting to take the various organs to hospitals all over town, where various transplant operations were in progress.

I walked into the theatre with the liver. As opposed to the public perception of theatres, a liver transplant always reminded me of Central Station. There was a hive of activity throughout the complex, with technicians carrying vials of blood, plasma and medications, moving equipment backwards and forwards to the various laboratories in the hospital. The cost to the taxpayer could only be measured in hundreds of thousands of dollars.

'He was drunk when he came in! Can you believe we're even doing this?' It was Sanchez again. Schumacher shot her a murderous look. I was too tired to care.

'The liver is in fine shape, Ryan. Young kid, motorbike. No contusions. Good match.' I spoke to Schumacher without him looking up.

'Why don't you scrub in?' This was not an invitation. This was an order.

'Have you had any sleep?' Sanchez was strictly by-the-book. She was on the resident medical officers' working party for safe working hours. This was an attempt to ensure that residents did not work in excess of 80 hours per week and that they had enough sleep between shifts. The AMA had also supported the issue and was insisting on abolishing the 56-hour shifts that we routinely did as surgical registrars.

'Yeah, I am fine.' I would be a wimp otherwise. My career would be marred if I showed a lack of willingness to take up an opportunity to assist Professor Ryan Schumacher with this transplant. This was a career-making invitation to join the inner sanctum. Scrubbing on a liver transplant was a great honour.

Twelve hours later, I un-scrubbed, wrote up the notes and saw Justice Connolly to the ICU.

The transplant had gone well. Within four weeks he was back home with normal colour returning to him. He was no longer the bright yellow ochre that was the hallmark of liver failure. Everyone was sure that he would continue drinking. I wondered how long it would be before we saw him again for the second transplant.

As for my transplant career, I abandoned it before it had commenced. Schumacher was supportive, but transplantation as a field had not inspired me.

CHAPTER 11
Working Holiday

Should auld acquaintance be forgot,
And never brought to mind?
Should auld acquaintance be forgot,
And auld lang syne?
For auld lang syne, my dear,
For auld lang syne,
We'll take a cup o' kindness yet,
For auld lang syne.

'AULD LANG SYNE' BY ROBERT BURNS

Tinsel livens up even the dullest of places. Every Christmas and New Year, in hospitals around the world, boxes of tinsel that have been stored in the Charge Sister's cupboard for the previous eleven months are brought out and stuck to the walls with bits of Blu Tack and Sellotape, or even hospital dressings – an attempt to mask the awful tragedies they witness. It always looks odd. Despite the best intentions of the tinsel addicts, the result is invariably that of dressing up an old hag's face with white powder and rouge, red lipstick and blue eyeliner. To those of us who are stuck with working over Christmas and New Year, it is a hateful time.

My first year as a surgical registrar was nearing its end and it was the honour of every first-year registrar to be on call for Christmas and New Year. It would be several years before I could enjoy the festive season at home with my wife. We had both decided not to have children until our training was over. Only her family was interested in celebrating Christmas – mine did not even recognise it as a holiday.

For doctors, it was often easier to be at work than to celebrate happy events at home. When a doctor is at home, the celebrations of those around them who are unaware of the hell zone in which they spend the majority of their life irritates, and causes them to rebel against the joy. A son's face as he opens presents reminds the doctor of the parents in the hospital whose Christmas is about wondering whether their son will see New Year. A mother opening her brand-new nightgown reminds the doctor of the nightdress of the lady who died that morning. It is difficult to know whether it is easier to work and be on call or to have the time off. I preferred to work.

New Year's Eve was more bearable. At least Christmas was over and the only thing to cope with was whether or not

I would be in theatre, operating at the stroke of midnight, or whether I would be able to see the fireworks. I spent this particular New Year's Eve, once again, in theatres.

Mr Towalavoa, a Fijian man of gigantic proportions, had been standing on the train platform with a blood alcohol level of 0.15 (three times the legal limit for driving). It is not known whether he tripped or fainted or was pushed, however, about three seconds before the train was due to pass the exact spot where he had been standing, Joe, as his friends called him, lay sprawled on the tracks. His right hip and left knee were suddenly spread-eagled across one line and his left elbow was across the other.

Bystanders were shouting to him to get off the track. The driver had seen him fall and was now facing his biggest nightmare of trying to stop before he ran over a man who had appeared out of nowhere on the tracks in front of him. No one had time to do anything, of course, apart from shout and look horrified. The train slowed down rapidly, but not in time to prevent the crush amputation of Joe Towalavoa's right leg across the hip, exposing his bladder and bowel, his left leg above the knee and his arm from above the elbow.

When he arrived into hospital, he had lost about 40 per cent of his blood volume and had arrested twice in the ambulance. He was intubated and colloidal fluid was being infused at a rapid rate via two cannulas – one in his right arm and the other in his neck. The trauma surgeon was already doing a primary survey.

The anaesthetic registrar was now putting in large bore cannulas so that blood could be infused and I was trying to insert a catheter into his bladder. He had lost part of his scrotum and the tip of his penis and so the best way was to insert the catheter directly through his abdominal wound into the bladder and sew it in place. I thought about local anaesthetic, but Joe was well and truly unconscious.

'Respiratory arrest! Who's free?' yelled the triage nurse as she came round the corner with another patient on a gurney – a 25-year-old transvestite who had overdosed on narcotics. She/he had taken so much heroin that his/her breathing had stopped. Collapsed in the middle of the street in the red-light district, passers-by had risked their lives giving mouth-to-mouth resuscitation while waiting for an ambulance. Maggie D'Souza, as he called himself, was HIV positive. I left Joe to attend to Maggie. The paramedics continued to bag her (pump oxygen into her lungs), and I got the Narcan.

Narcan is a miracle drug for narcotic overdoses. The patient usually wakes up before the needle is emptied. Maggie started to stir. I had given her a large dose.

'Don't give me more, you fuck-wit,' she screamed. Her right hand came up with fist clenched and swung fiercely at me, connecting with my chest and hitting the triage sister on the rebound. The sister swung around, her nose already bleeding. I went to her aid.

'Are you OK?' I said.

'Yeah, I'm fine. I should've known better. It's not the first time we've seen Maggie. He's a bastard.' She was putting pressure on her nose to stem the bleeding.

I turned to see Maggie disconnecting all the cannulas and staggering to the exit.

'Come on, mate, you need more Narcan, you'll just stop breathing again.'

I was trying to hold him back. He swung at me again.

'Go get fucked! Do you know how much heroin costs? Fuck off and leave me alone. You didn't have to use so much Narcan.'

The overdosers all knew about Narcan. He was livid. I let him go.

'Cardiac arrest!'

Joe was busy trying to die. He had lost even more blood and the anaesthetic registrar was unable to put a cannula in to replace the blood at a sufficiently fast volume. The trauma surgeon had opened his chest through a slash on the left side, obliquely between the fourth and fifth rib spaces, and had his hand in Joe's chest, pumping his heart for him. His forearm muscles were rippling with the effort of squeezing his fist around the man's heart, which in itself was about the size of the anaesthetic registrar's fist.

This was always a last-ditch effort. The mess was extreme. Blood streamed onto the floor of the casualty department. We were wading in blood and soaked bandages. Add to that the unmistakable smell of innards, open flesh, muscles that have been crushed, bowel. All of them have a distinct smell that pervades the senses – a constant reminder for the rest of the day. Joe was dead really, we were only going through the motions. A pulse came back momentarily.

'We have sinus rhythm,' screamed the trauma surgeon.

Not for long, I thought.

The triage sister came up to me. 'Maggie's back. He collapsed at the front gate of the hospital,' she said, without resentment or disappointment.

Maggie was not breathing. Because it was New Year, we were down to a skeleton staff. No one had discovered him for twenty minutes. The brain can take only three minutes without oxygen. I felt his carotid pulse. Gone. I started cardiac resuscitation.

'Get me a tube and take over on the chest!' I shouted.

A tube was handed to me and I tilted the head back, placed the scope down so that I could image the larynx and then slipped a tracheal tube into the trachea, connected it to a bag and started respiratory action. The cardiac massage was being administered by Judy, a very attractive junior nurse. The idea was to rock backwards and forwards using your weight to compress the heart between the front of the chest and the vertebral column so that blood is pumped around the body and, most importantly, to the brain, mimicking a normal heart rate of about 80 beats per minute. It's the same rate that most mothers rock their babies and the average rate that men thrust pelvically during sex.

Tonight, the bed was squeaking. Each time Judy rocked forwards, it squeaked like the bed of troublesome neighbours in a cheap hotel. She had a large battery-operated Christmas tree pinned to her left breast, which lit up in four different-coloured LED lights powered by hearing-aid batteries. Her ample breasts bounced up and down. Maggie was vomiting. I suctioned her vomit up and continued to watch the cardiac massage.

The triage nurse, Lillian, and I were transfixed by the sight of this beauteous young girl, earnest in her attempts to resuscitate this half-man, half-woman, putting her heart and soul into her life-saving. Maggie was dead. Neither Lillian nor I wanted to call it. The rocking of the breasts with the coloured lights blinking in tandem, the squeaking of the bed, the grunting of the young nubile nurse – it was a scene straight out of a Fellini film. If one were to have frozen the moment in time it would've inspired a Dalí masterpiece.

My beeper went off, jarring me out of the whole scene. Theatre. I looked up at the clock.

'Time of death: 11.45 pm. I'll come back and do the paperwork later,' I said as I left to go to theatre.

Judy continued to pump the chest. I looked back to see Lillian take her hand and explain that she could stop now – the doctor had declared death.

This would be the fourth year in a row that I would not see the fireworks. All over the city, lives were being ripped apart. Car accidents, overdoses, functioning retards given power tools as Christmas presents, drownings and, most of all, suicides.

Christmas and the New Year were the high watermarks for suicides. Spending these festive days alone was too much for many. Suicide presented the only alternative to a lonely life brought into stark contrast with the advertising campaigns of happy families getting presents, the reruns of *Miracle on 49th Street* and the constant maddening drone of well-wishers. A Salvation Army food pack didn't quite make up for the feeling of being totally rejected by society and family. We saw them all here in the hospital for the holiday season and patched up the lives of those whose body gave them an opportunity to have a little company, even if the company was five patients, the nurses and an attending physician. It was better than nobody.

Jack Johnson, the senior registrar on call, was up in theatre with a dead bowel. A 90-year-old lady had been in hospital with vague abdominal pain and a low-grade temperature – symptoms that could easily be confused with a urinary tract infection or a viral illness. Twice her family doctor had sent her home, but a week ago she was brought into casualty by her daughter when she failed to get any better. Eventually, she started to look more septic. Her white-cell count was down, indicating an overwhelming infection. That can only come from one place: the abdomen.

Jack decided to take her to theatre for a laparotomy, an exploratory operation of the abdomen. The incision goes from just below the chest all the way down to the pubic bone. The older surgeons used to pride themselves on opening the abdomen in one swoop, one incision. It was a point of pride, of dexterity, of skill.

These days, because of the large incidence of bowel perforations from the 'older surgeons', we opened the abdomen in layers. Jack was meticulous: skin, subcutaneous tissue and the abdominal fascia, carefully lift up the peritoneum and then into the abdomen itself. That's when the smell hits you. This lady had dead gut. You smell it way before you see it. There was blood mixed in with the abdominal fluid. We confirmed this with a quick look around and then closed up.

'She's fucked,' said Jack.

'Yeah, poor lady,' I replied, and yawned. My need for sleep had overtaken any form of human feeling at the passing of another. When you are surrounded by death it is hard to get excited about yet another one. This woman had raised a family, had a lifetime of memories, had defended her country during the Great War and had lived to see great-grandchildren born. Her demise was to come in an unfamiliar hospital, tended to by two strangers whose skills and expertise could not extend her life, a life destined to a desultory end as the toxins from the dead bowel in her abdomen circulated throughout her system and overwhelmed her vital functions. We had tried but there was no cure.

I had several other deaths to document that night and every night. Most deaths brought with them an outpouring of grief from those who would miss them dearly. Some deaths were not like that – they would pass alone and unnoticed.

Either way, for us, it was just another number, another patient, another name off the long list of names on the board waiting for an operation. Were I to stop and grieve each passing life, I would become ineffectual. I would become paralysed by grief, unable to provide my skills as a technician without fear, boldly plunging a knife into people in order to save them from their rotting bodies. Perhaps for a surgeon, dwelling on death is akin to a tightrope walker looking down instead of straight ahead, or a toreador dwelling upon the beast's horns before a bullfight.

Society needs technically competent, brave, even arrogant surgeons whose strength is derived from perfecting the craft. Perhaps for Jack and me, our callous disregard for this death was a necessary part of our survival. Or perhaps surgery was blunting my humanity.

'I'm fine here. Do you want to go see if there is any family?' Jack always hated to tell the family bad news. I un-scrubbed and looked up at the clock. It was 12.20 am.

'Hey, Happy New Year, Jack!' I mustered some enthusiasm.

He looked up at me and the clock.

'Yeah, you too. Hey, have we missed the fireworks again. Ah, fuck it!'

CHAPTER 12

A Successful Clone

Death, be not proud, though some have called thee
Mighty and dreadful, for thou art not so:
For those whom thou think'st thou dost overthrow
Die not, poor Death; nor yet canst thou kill me.
From Rest and Sleep, which but thy picture be,
Much pleasure, then from thee much more must flow;
And soonest our best men with thee do go –
Rest of their bones and souls' delivery!
Thou'rt slave to fate, chance, kings, and desperate men,
And dost with poison, war, and sickness dwell;
And poppy or charms can make us sleep as well
And better than thy stroke. Why swell'st thou then?
One short sleep past, we wake eternally,
And Death shall be no more: Death, thou shalt die!

'DEATH' BY JOHN DONNE

Apart from the excruciatingly long hours we worked each week as a surgical registrar, we were expected to study, prepare for talks at a rate of one a month, and do some research. As each year progressed, our responsibilities increased and the operations I performed became increasingly more complex. I struggled to finish writing my doctorate. I finally did so by giving up my annual holidays and checking into a motel near our home. I moved in with 16 boxes of data, research findings and papers. Ten days later my thesis was written. I went back to work the next day.

As a registrar, I spent my life juggling work activities with fundamental bodily requirements and functions such as eating, sleeping and eliminating waste. There was never time to go to the bank, think about finance, read the newspaper, take a walk in the garden, engage in deep conversation, go to a gallery – the list is endless. Occasionally you attempted to socialise, visit a concert or a dinner, but it was most unlikely that you would stay awake after the entrée or past the first act.

The only people that you interacted with were medical people – doctors and nurses. You usually ended up married to one of these people, as I had. They were the only ones who had a chance of understanding the demands of your job. A couple of years later, even they ceased to understand and they divorced you, allowing the cycle to start again. Some held on to their sanity amid the chaos. Others became manic.

Superimposed over this training scheme was your ordinary life – parents and friends, bills that need paying, calls that need returning. By the end of your training, you were inevitably alone. Your parents may have died or retired somewhere, your friends had grown away and pleasant chitchat bored you anyway. Financially, you were a disaster, and socially you were inept. And you didn't know it. You were still king of all you surveyed. The thrill of taking the scalpel in your hand was still fresh in your narrow, life-starved mind. However, you were a bore. You once played the violin or the occasional round of golf. You were once an avid reader; now you couldn't remember the last time you devoured a good book. You vaguely remembered when you were once the life of the party.

The final exam in surgery loomed large and your only chance of success was total, exclusionist dedication. It was too late to trouble yourself with thoughts of developing into a Renaissance man or woman now. There was only one goal: fellowship. Crossing the barrier from touchable to untouchable. Gaining the locus of control – self-determination.

Having completed several years of surgical training, it was time to do the specialty examination. I was now in my third year of training as a urologist. The exam was conducted in this, the final year of specialist training. It was comprised of two sections. There was a one-day written exam that tested clinical judgement and a knowledge of the literature in your specialty. Then there were three gruelling days of *viva voce* – detailed anatomy and embryology, pathology, operative science, clinical judgement and anything else the examiner felt was fair on the day of examination. This was not just an examination of knowledge but about your acceptance into a college of like-minded individuals. It was about who you were as a surgeon. Where you stood. Were you suitable? Had the cloning process been a success? Were there any chinks in the armour? Had all individuality been buried alive?

The final product of training was a clone of the expectations and desires of a surgical college that has changed little since its inception in the sixteenth century. The expectations were ephemeral, and yet all who played the game success-fully seemed somehow to know what was expected. You hid yourself from view for fear that there were characteristics about yourself that would discount you from becoming part of the club. After a while I was able to don the outward manifestation of upper-middle-class Western conservatism as easily as I could don my theatre attire.

Each *viva voce* took thirty minutes. Two examiners, one candidate. The examiners were humans so they were aware of all the foibles, innuendos and rumours about you and the mistakes you had made during your training. Often, they were surgeons you had trained with, people who had seen you at your worst and your best.

Traditions that have survived from the eighteenth century are still employed to add to the sense of awe and occasion. The examiners wore the coloured silk-lined robes worn by Fellows of the College, as if to say, 'We are members and you are not.' Not yet, anyway.

On the final day of examination the candidates assem-bled in the foyer of the College of Surgeons to get their results. There was so much adrenaline flowing in this room that you could almost smell it in the air. After what seemed to be an interminable length of time, the registrar of the College appeared and read the candidates' numbers. You walked up past all the other surgical registrars who had just completed the gruelling ordeal of the fellowship examina-tion and picked up your envelope. It was best not to rush, and best not to open the envelope with anyone else lest you betrayed your feelings of disappointment when you failed. The envelope contains a single white card. On the card, below the crest of the College, was typed one of two sentences: '*You have not been successful at this attempt*' or '*Congratulations, you have been successful*'.

Mine contained the latter.

Quiet elation was the best emotion under the circumstances. There were those around you with tears streaming down their faces – some of relief, others of disappointment. There were those who were angry and those to whom failure came as no surprise. There were the star trainees who had failed in an imperfect system. There was no natural justice here.

You were sent a short letter several weeks later to tell you where you failed in very general terms. There was no questioning the umpire.

Slowly, the failures – the have-nots – left the room and the successful candidates lined up in order to be presented to the court of examiners. The head examiner and the other examiners individually welcomed each candidate in turn.

Drinks were then served. Traditionally, sherry was taken. Even I, for a few minutes, felt a sense of belonging. I had reached a goal towards which I had strived for the first 33 years of my life. At that moment, all the pain and suffering was worth it; the sense of victory was complete.

*

Now the journey really started for me. I was once again at the start of another phase. I had been offered an appointment at the Victoria Hospital, which was dependent on me passing this examination. Waiting for me was the world of private surgery. I was now a 'boss'.

The next time I walked into a hospital would be as a surgeon. I had achieved my lifelong ambition, the ambition I had held from the age of three, when I spent hours operating on teddy bears. I clung to the dream throughout high school and then the five years as a medical student, the internship year, the three years of residency, and finally the five years on the advanced surgical registrar training scheme – it had all come to an end.

I was in my mid-thirties and life was about to begin. Utter elation – the type that Olympic sprinters exhibit when they win the gold medal – washed over me. Elation and relief. But the elation soon gave way to a deep sense of fright. I was now expected to take full responsibility. I was expected to make the final decisions. There was no reliance on another. I was the final arbiter of life and death. What I did with my hands and my mind affected all that were in the position to be my patients. *My patients.*

I gazed around the room at the portraits of past Presidents of the College that adorned the walls and realised that I was now their colleague. Perez, Nordstrom, Schumacher were now my colleagues. That too filled me with fright. Could I measure up to the expectations?

I was well-trained. I was competent. The examination had just testified to that. Yet the sense of inadequateness could not be shaken. That evening, as I sat at a celebratory dinner with my wife, I realised, now more than ever, I needed her. I needed the comfort, the understanding, the compassion that only she could offer. I resisted a large number of dinners that had been planned, and celebrated my achievement only with her – the only one who truly mattered.

Yet I did not feel like we were alone at the dinner table. Beside her were sitting the images of the tens of surgeons who had made *me* a surgeon. From my first operation until my last day as a registrar, I had been guided, supported, humiliated, taught and mentored, with a generosity of spirit that is rare in any other profession. To this day, surgeons teach without payment. They pass on their skills to their wards with a parental need to see the generations improve and keep alive the spirit of surgery, of Aesculapius, of Ibn-Sina and of the countless greats that have paved the craggy mountain laneway that is Surgery.

I was continuing a tradition and not just getting a ticket to practice. We operate safely today because of the greatness of surgeons like Semmelweis and Lister, the genius of Cushing and the courage of Halsted.

A good surgeon, Halsted said, 'has the eyes of an eagle, the hands of a woman, the heart of a lion and a mind like a steel trap'.

Somehow, I felt like I had the heart of a wimp and the hands of a lion, and eyes that could hardly focus with the excitement of anticipation.

Ultimately, becoming a surgeon is a transparent process, which is still best described as an apprenticeship rather than a formal training. You start by holding a retractor as a junior resident. By a process akin to osmosis, you slowly absorb techniques, cutting sutures, showing the operator the field, closing. One day you are actually allowed to cut the sutures. Inevitably, you use the belly of the scissors rather than the tips. You are shown the correct way. Sometime later you get to put in your first sutures; this involves recognising which layers to sew together. If you can cut you can dissect. If you can close a wound you can tie a knot in a blood vessel. These are the two fundamental tools of surgery: cutting and sewing. Then comes your first skin excision, your first appendix, your first gall bladder, and you realise one day that you have become a surgeon. All that is lacking is experience and wisdom.

Wisdom comes from good judgement, and good judgement comes from learning each time you make a bad judgement. The good, publicly insured, indigent people of the world allow you to make your bad judgements on them so that when you have fee-paying, privately insured patients, you usually make good judgements.

In years to come, good judgement will be learned by killing several virtual patients in a computer simulation. The tie comes off because you took too much tissue. You decide to use a right iliac fossa incision for an appendix and the patient turns out to have a caecal carcinoma instead. You dissect a small structure in the retroperitoneal space and decide it is fibrous, and when you cut it, urine exudes from the cut ends. All of this and more will be practised in simulations, wearing goggles with realistic visual inputs and gloves that allow us to be fooled into thinking we are operating on human flesh.

Virtual reality will remain an intellectual exercise until the technology allows it to become the chosen and correct way of surgical training. Until then, the poor will continue to serve the rich in being living laboratories for doctors to learn on.

My wife sat opposite me, quietly allowing me to be absorbed in my thoughts. I looked at her overgrown abdomen full of our first child. My thoughts turned to my impending fatherhood.

A few months later, my first boy was born. No two events in my life, before or since, have or will rival the day my first son was born and, a year later, the day when my second son came into this world. With them came a heart-bursting joy and a gravity of responsibility.

Here was something far more important to me than surgery.

My family.

PART TWO
Practice

CHAPTER 13
Ode on Solitude

Happy the man whose wish and care
A few paternal acres bound,
Content to breathe his native air
In his own ground.
Whose herds with milk, whose fields with bread,
Whose flocks supply him with attire,
Whose trees in summer yield him shade,
In winter fire.
Blest, who can unconcern'dly find
Hours, days, and years, slide soft away,
In health of body, peace of mind,
Quiet by day,
Sound sleep by night, study and ease
Together mixed, sweet recreation,
And innocence, which most does please,
With meditation.
Thus let me live, unseen, unknown,
Thus unlamented let me die;
Steal from the world, and not a stone
Tell where I lie.

'ODE ON SOLITUDE' BY ALEXANDER POPE

'There is the Science of Surgery, the Art of Surgery and then there is the Business of Surgery. You have learned the first two. You have now to learn the Business of Surgery.'

These were the words of wisdom I was given on my last day of surgical training by one of my colleagues. His words resounded in my mind as I geared up for my first private consulting list in my own rooms.

I had at long last finished my training and I had an appointment as a Visiting Medical Officer at the Victoria Hospital. This was indeed an honour. It was difficult to get these appointments. There had been 20 other candidates for my position, each with their Fellowship and each with a good CV. I had planned ahead though. I had a string of research papers, a doctorate and degrees in computing and education. I had become more and more interested in computer-assisted learning in surgery during my residency years and had completed my computer degree. During my research year, I enrolled in and finished a Masters of Education. Perhaps, even then, I nurtured quiet ambitions of becoming an academic. I would often keep these degrees from my colleagues as I felt they thought I was slightly mad.

Those who did know would ask, 'Why would you subject yourself to doing part-time degrees when we hardly ever get out of the hospital?'

Perhaps I was a sucker for punishment. I have always had a capacity for work. Those degrees won the day for me by securing my appointment. More importantly, I was genuinely interested in the field of education, though I would not have an opportunity to put my knowledge to use until much later.

The investment in opening rooms is huge. There is an outlay of several tens of thousands of dollars on equipment, examination couches, waiting-room chairs, gloves. I had to hire staff – a secretary was the minimum. Most importantly, one had to let the family practitioners know the practice was open. My secretary and I sat down with the phone book and transcribed each relevant name and address. We sent letters out that described my training and the services we hoped to provide. We then followed up with phone calls to the practice to see if we could set up times to meet the referring doctor face to face.

Your practice lived or died by referring doctors. If they sent you patients then you had a practice. No patients – no practice. Good general practitioners are worth their weight in gold – however, the funding structure and various government cutbacks has meant that they can only survive by volume.

Extensive consultations have become an unaffordable activity. Thinking is an unaffordable activity. Medical centres thrive by volume and by over-servicing. Kickbacks, benefits and additional profits come from ordering tests. Apart from that, there is no money in being a general practitioner.

The colleges that credential family medicine, as it is sometimes called, live in the clouds, far and away from the reality of paying rent, wages and medical insurance. The overheads are so high that, as a general practitioner, it is often said you work until Thursday each week before you start making any money.

'Hello, my name is Mohamed Khadra and I am a new urologist. I would like to introduce my services to you . . . Sure . . . I am sorry, I did not realise you already refer to him. Could I perhaps leave my card with your secretary and if there are patients you have that may be suited for referral to me, I would love to see them . . . thanks for your time.'

It was devastating. As a registrar, you did not battle for patients. In the hospital, the 'boss' – the specialist for whom I worked, provided all the patients. Now I had to find them. I had to hunt for the cases and bring them in.

Advertising was broadly frowned upon. Plastic surgeons advertised. Urologists and other surgeons saw it as beneath them. It was still not accepted practice. Referral practices were set and it was hard to break in.

Doctors with migrant names were assumed to have trained overseas. Egypt or India was the most common sources of migrant doctors. The two countries with the greatest need for good healthcare seemed to be the ones exporting most of their precious commodity – people with skills. It was immoral to think that in any Western city, the ratio of doctors to the population can be as high as 1:500 when the ratio in countries with the greatest need can reach 1:100,000.

Yet the barrage of migrant doctors seeking a better economic life in the West continues unabated. Some are well-trained. Others are diabolically dangerous. The Government seems to have a wavering and alternating view of support or condemnation for these doctors. When there are complaints from rural areas in the West that there are relative shortages of doctors, the government increases the quota of migrant doctors that can be given licenses. It is a great solution for the government – 'doctors on tap' to be injected into the healthcare system as the need arises. Every now and then stories surface in the media of inappropriate or even dangerous practice by these doctors.

There have been doctors who have high complication rates. One committed a young patient in the rural north to a mental asylum because the doctor alleged the boy thought he was a kangaroo. In reality, the boy was telling the doctor that he worked as a jackeroo – a cow musterer. There was the conservative religious doctor who rejected giving a young 17-year-old girl pregnancy prevention advice and telling her that if she had sex before marriage all the boys would think she was a slut and her chances of getting married would be impossible.

Whenever I fronted up to a referring doctor and introduced myself, I felt like I had to prove my credentials, I had to establish my credibility, I had to overcome an assumption of incompetence that was brought about by me having the name Mohamed Khadra from birth.

I felt like saying 'I truly am competent'; 'My complication rate is really low'; 'I can take a bladder out in two and a half hours'; 'After a prostate resection, my patients go home on day five'.

Instead, I waited.

Each day, I would call my secretary. 'Any referrals?'

'No. Not yet. But it will come. Don't worry,' she would say cheerfully. Her salary had to be paid no matter what. I needed the referrals.

Consultations paid very little. You had to get the surgical operations in private practice to make money. A consultation went for about $100. I needed a lot of them to make up for the overhead that drained money out of my practice each week. How was I to get that many patients unless each of them needed an operation? Operations: that's where you made the money.

'There is the Science of Surgery, the Art of Surgery, and then there is the Business of Surgery.' These words came back to me over and over again.

My first patient was a young boy of sixteen. His referral letter was difficult to read. I was nervous. I reassured myself that I was competent for the task. I had resuscitated trauma victims in the middle of the night. I had diagnosed rare diseases and published an extensive array of articles and papers. There was very little I could not cope with. I was in fact looking forward to a really good case to establish my reputation.

I welcomed the boy into my brand-new consulting suite. I could not wait for the secretary to finish typing in his details on the computer's patient-record tracking system.

In he came, and sat down.

I focused again on the referral letter that was written on the back of a prescription pad. It read: 'Dear Dr Khadra, please see Daniel with scrotal problems.'

My mind raced with excitement. Could this be a testicular cancer? Ideally it would be a nonseminoma, the type that needed a retroperitoneal dissection to clear the nodes. I fixed the boy in my sight, putting on my most compassionate face.

'Your doctor tells me you're having problems down in your groin area,' I said in overly professional tones.

'Yeah, it's me balls,' he said. He was nonchalant, disengaged, unexcited.

'What is the problem with them?'

'One hangs down longer than the other.' He was quite earnest about this.

I repeated his symptoms slowly in disbelief. 'One . . . hangs lower . . . than the other? That's it? Do you have a mass, a tumour?'

'Nah, nothin' like that. It's just that one hangs lower than the other.' He was not really concerned.

It was almost impossible to get information from this boy. He could work for an intelligence organisation, except that intelligence and this boy were not to be used in the same sentence.

'Did your family doctor examine you before he sent you to see me?' I asked casually. I was getting frustrated. I was now almost hoping that he did have cancer.

'Nah. I just told him that one of me balls hangs down lower than the other and he said I should see a specialist. So then me mum made this appointment.'

More words than I had extracted from him during the entire consultation.

'OK, mate. Let us have a look.' I got him up on the brand-new $4500 examination couch. He lay down with his muddy sneakers on the burgundy coloured leather. I looked in disgust at his shoes. He did not pick up on my obvious torture. He lay back, looking up at the ceiling. He was wearing board shorts, a T-shirt, and about ten of those coloured rubber bands that young people seemed to be buying in abundance as a decorative item.

'I need you to pull your shorts down so that I can examine your scrotum,' I said. I could see I had better clarify. 'Your ball-bag. Your balls, mate.'

He was absolutely clear by now about what had to be done. He slipped down his shorts and exposed his genitals.

I felt his scrotum overall, then his left testicle and then his right testicle; his epididymis, his spermatic cord; the skin of the scrotum and then the penis. I retracted his foreskin. He needed a shower.

'That all seems in good order. There are no problems here. Now I need you to stand up,' I said.

He stood up with his pants around his ankles.

'Give me a cough.' I placed my fingers up his hernial orifices. Not even a hernia.

'Now get dressed and come and sit down and we can chat,' I said, playing the consummate professional.

I reassured him that it was perfectly normal to have one ball hanging down lower than the other. I reassured him he did not have cancer or any life-threatening, i.e. 'paying' condition. I dictated a nice letter to his family doctor. I left out the bits that I truly wanted to say, such as, 'Look here, you incompetent prick. If you ever send me another patient with nothing wrong I will have you struck off!'

I hated referrals of this kind. They spoke more about the ignorance and carelessness of some general practitioners than about any assessment of the patient prior to special- ist referral. They were disrespectful and mechanical. Some general practitioners abrogate all thought to the specialist. They do not use their medical training to get to the heart of a problem and assess the need for special- ist intervention. They are little more than the triage nurses working in most casualty departments in hospitals. Their job is to work out which department in the hospital the patient needs to go to. A quick bandage on the gushing bleeder and then wait for the resident to do the needful. 'Do the needful' is another thoughtless referral specialists get all the time.

'Abdominal pain. Please assess and do the needful.'

I had to wait another week for my second patient. This time the referral read, 'Please see Paul for ejaculatory concerns.' I recognised that it was the same referring doctor even before I read the note. It was written on the back of a prescription pad. My heart sank.

Paul's complaint was that he was not having wet dreams. His friend had wet dreams, but he did not. I asked him if he masturbated. After looking very embarrassed and sheepish for about 30 seconds, he admitted that he wanked not more than twice a day.

I reassured him that wet dreams were a safety-valve mechanism to release built-up semen, and if he wanted wet dreams then he had to give up masturbation. This was a tough decision, which he could ponder.

The next patient for the day was a paranoid schizophrenic who was concerned about the size of his genitals. Having a sexual fixation of some description is not uncommon for schizophrenic patients.

'I have a tic-tac and two peanuts,' he blurted.

'Well, let us have a look, shall we?' I was turning into a smarmy surgeon and I hated it. I had not done an operation for some weeks. It was really starting to get me panicked. I got him up on the examination couch. He pulled down his pants and lifted his head upwards so that he looked in the opposite direction to his genitals. He did not wish to see them or even catch a glimpse of them.

I examined his genitals sequentially and methodically. Left testicle, right testicle, cord, skin, penis.

'Mate, let me tell you the truth. I would be proud to have genitals as big or as perfect as these,' I said with an absolutely straight face.

'Are you telling me that this is normal? Small prick and balls is normal?' He looked ferocious, unhappy with my lack of absolute conviction in a diagnosis of inadequacy.

'Normal. Absolutely normal,' I reassured him.

'Well, you are a fucking idiot! Someone said you were a trained specialist. You are nothing more than a fuckwit! You do not know what the fuck you are doing!' He got up, got dressed and went out, slamming the consultation door behind him.

I sat back in my chair. I was really exhausted. I had no patients to speak of. I had booked no operations. I was going broke.

I looked up at my degrees hanging on the wall. What was it all for – all the years that went into getting my doctorate? The hours and hours of sacrifice to get each of the letters after my name. This was not medicine, this was not what I signed up for. I wanted big, precedent-setting cases to sink my teeth into. I wanted to cure cancer. I wanted to heal the sick, bring the dead back to life. Instead, I was seeing what we euphemistically call the 'worried well'.

Suddenly, the door opened again.

'You do not expect me to pay this fucking bill here, do yah?' He was about to punch me.

'No, it's all right. Just leave.' I did not want to enter into a physical fight with this patient for payment. A bad debt is better than physical conflict in my rooms.

I waited a week before I was referred my next patient, a male with some difficulty passing urine. His urinary stream was somewhat diminished in the morning when he awoke, he had some hesitancy and the occasional urgency to quickly locate a toilet. Otherwise, he was well.

This is a very common story. It forms the 'bread and butter' of urological practice. Men have a gland that surrounds the opening to their bladder called the prostate. As men grow older their prostate gland continues to grow larger, mostly under the effect of testosterone that is the defining hormone of masculinity. This growth of the prostate can sometimes be due to benign enlargement or cancer.

Prostate cancer is the largest cause of death in adult males and, unfortunately, has become a highly politicised disease. A political disease is a disease where every stakeholder feels the need to make a public statement about the disease and their own views about how it should be managed and treated.

Old men (spurred on by urologists) want it screened for and discovered early. The logic was that screening for prostate cancer may result in earlier diagnosis of the disease and, hence, earlier treatment. This would save lives. Treatment for early cancer was surgery. No one knew whether early treatment actually did save lives. It is possible that by the time prostate cancer is diagnosed, the biological lifecycle is almost complete and the patient's fate is sealed.

The health economists did not buy the argument for screening because it is mostly old men who die from prostate cancer, hence the number of 'man years' that are saved from early diagnosis, if any, would be minimal in comparison to the cost of screening everyone and the impost placed on an already stretched health budget.

Medical oncologists did not want it diagnosed early because the treatment for late-stage cancer was chemotherapy or hormonal ablation, both treatments that could be performed by physicians. The oncologists' vested interest was in getting the patient late.

Scientists claimed that huge amounts of research dollars should be poured into research about prostate cancer so that we can understand the disease better and maybe even find a cure. The fiscal survival of scientists depended on research dollars.

No wonder patients found prostate cancer a confusing disease.

If prostate cancer is confusing, then benign prostatic obstruction is even more so. Benign prostate obstruction is the commonest condition we treat as urologists. Treatments range from doing nothing and reassuring the patient, to tablets and then all the way to surgery.

The operation, the transurethral resection of the prostate, called TURP by friends, is one of the most common operations. It pays well. More fortunes have been made from TURP operations than any other operation. Some patients absolutely needed an operation. Most patients could be left alone. In fact, the research is clear. Eighty per cent of patients get better or stay the same if observed over time. Only 20 per cent get worse. Yet, the vast majority of patients who turn up to an urologist with these lower urinary tract symptoms are likely to end up with an operation.

Herein lies the conflict of interest inherent in all private surgery. I had already started to find it unpalatable and I was only in my second month of private practice.

In front of me sat a 55-year-old male, Mr John James. His tests and examination had revealed to me that the cause of his prostate obstruction was benign in origin and could be treated with medications or even reassurance. If I recommended that course of action (albeit the correct course of action), I would earn about $100, or whatever it was that I charged for a consultation. If I recommended surgery, I would end up earning between $1500 and $5000, depending on how much I set my fee for a TURP.

I sat there, staring at all the findings in front of me. I had spent the afternoon trying to negotiate an overdraft with the bank. Some urologists earned millions. How did they do it? Was it by operating on patients who did not need operations?

'There is the Science of Surgery, the Art of Surgery, and then there is *the Business of Surgery*.'

Was that what was meant by 'the Business of Surgery'? I chose to believe that was not the case. I wanted to believe in an honourable surgical practice. That it was possible to make a living while remaining true to oneself.

By and large, the surgeons I knew were honourable people. Yet, if this was a corporation and I was a director, the conflict of interest would have to be declared. I would need to place this conflict of interest before the board.

I decided to do exactly that. I told Mr John James about benign prostate disease and about the various ways to treat it. I told him about the conflict of interest and how I believed he was the only one that could make the decision and the decision needed to be based on his symptoms. I told him about the likely outcomes if his prostate was not treated, and the likely outcomes if it was.

'Mr James, you do not need an operation unless your symptoms are so bad that you feel you would risk your life to improve them.' I thought I had to be honest and he needed to understand that a TURP had at least a potential to result in his death.

Patients do not like to think that even the most minor of operations can result in death as a complication. Mr John James sat there, confused and bewildered. He edged out of my rooms, indicating that he would like to think about it.

Two weeks later, my colleague was doing Mr John James's TURP in the private hospital.

CHAPTER 14

Into the Sunset

All devil as I am – a damned wretch,
A hardened, stubborn, unrepenting villain,
Still my heart melts at human wretchedness;
And with sincere but unavailing sighs
I view the helpless children of distress:
With tears indignant I behold the oppressor
Rejoicing in the honest man's destruction,
Whose unsubmitting heart was all his crime.
Ev'n you, ye hapless crew! I pity you;
Ye, whom the seeming good think sin to pity;
Ye poor, despised, abandoned vagabonds,
Whom Vice, as usual, has turn'd o'er to ruin.

'TRAGIC FRAGMENT' BY ROBERT BURNS

Impotence is a strange affliction. A lack of confidence is the basis for 80 per cent of men who suffer from impotence. They will fail to perform once, say, after a long day at work or during a drinking binge, and then the next time they'll have sex, they can think of nothing but whether or not they are going to perform. Of course, they fail. This fuels their belief that they are now 'IMPOTENT'. The word seems to strike terror in their hearts and they suddenly find it impossible to face their wives and partners. They shun sex. It is a self-fulfilling prophecy and a spiral that is the cause of great unhappiness to middle-aged men.

My approach to impotence was to do a series of tests to ensure that the patient did not have one of the more rare forms of impotence caused by some underlying disease: atherosclerosis, diabetes, multiple sclerosis, etc., etc., etc. The vast majority had nothing irreversible. Once they were reassured about this, we commenced a treatment regime that included discussing the issues with their partner present.

The partner wants to know that the man does not have cancer and is not going to die. They love them not because they can have a big hard-on but because of so many other reasons that have nothing to do with their penis. This is difficult for the majority of men to understand. 'There is something about me worth loving other than my cock?'

I'd talk about alternatives to penetrative sex. Then, I'd talk about the various medications that have revolutionised erectile dysfunction. Finally, when all else fails and they were desperate to have an erection, we talked about operations.

These operations used to be commonplace before Viagra, Cialis and Levitra – the anti-impotence drugs that solve the problem for the majority of men. Now, operations are reserved for those for whom all else fails.

The operation consists of placing a silicon-coated rod into the substance of the penis. There are three models.

The Mini Minor is the cheapest and consists of a silicon-coated silver rod that is implanted into the penis and gives the patient a constant erection. When they want to have sexual intercourse they bend it forward and into 'action'. The rest of the time they dress themselves to one side or the other.

The Family Sedan is moderately expensive. A silicon tube is implanted behind the bladder that is inflated with fluid from a reservoir. The head of the penis is pumped up and the silicon stiffens to give a semi-erect penis. Once the sexual act is complete, the head of the penis is squeezed again and the tube deflates.

The Rolls-Royce is the ultimate in penile technology. It consists of three parts, each of which is implanted in a separate place. The tubing is in the penis, the pump in the scrotum next to the testis and the reservoir behind the bladder. This model, when pumped, increases in length and girth!

Abdullah sat opposite me, tensely, and with an obvious impatience to tell me his story. He was proud that I was Lebanese like him, and this gave him a comfort and a kinship that allowed him to speak freely.

'You know, I used to be able to lift this desk with my prick.' He was serious.

'So how about now?' I was fascinated.

'I cannot do it any more. Ever since I turned 63. I am really worried, Doctor.' He was very serious about this matter.

'But, let me get this straight. You can still have sexual intercourse? You are able to penetrate your penis into her vagina. Is that right?' I wanted to understand the gravity of his dysfunction.

'Yessss. What do you take me for? I have not turned into a woman. It is just that it is not as strong as it used to be.'

He was really concerned about his erectile state and I ended up spending the next hour explaining the mechanism of an erection and reassuring him that he was normal and needed no treatment.

I opened the notes for a new patient. 'Please see for erection problems.' I went out to the waiting room. 'Jack Ignatius,' I called.

I detested Jack from the start. He came into my office wearing a black silk shirt and heavy gold chains and a bracelet. He looked evil and yet I could not pin down the evil. Perhaps it was just my imagination playing tricks with me after a long day.

'How are ya, Doc?' Broad Australian accent.

'Yeah, good. What can I do for you?'

Ockerism returned. 'I have had troubles getting it up lately, Doc. Not all the time. Just sometimes. A man can't live with this type of problem.'

So I went into the patter of erectile dysfunction assessment. Are you diabetic? Is there any neurological damage? Is there a hormonal problem? Is there a psychological problem? History, examination, investigations.

'I am going to arrange a few tests to make sure we know what we are dealing with,' I said listlessly.

'But I've already had heaps of bloody tests from Tom!'

I hated it when patients called their doctor by the first name, as if they were a long-lost friend or a member of the family. Some doctors felt it broke down barriers. I believe the barriers are useful: they establish roles. They establish who is in charge. There are times when that barrier and authority is all you have to manage a patient who is noncompliant with treatment. Why take away one of the most significant lines of defence?

'Can you give me anything in the meantime, Doc?'

I began to hate the term 'Doc'.

'It is best if we wait for the results and make sure that there is nothing serious underlying your erection problems. The vast majority of cases are treatable. Just be patient with me. We should have these results back within a few days and I will see you next week.' I wanted him out of my practice.

As I drove home, I began having nasty images of those heavy chains hanging around my own neck and that big gold bracelet on my wrist, but quickly dismissed the thought as I narrowly avoided a rather large truck from ploughing into the back of my car. A sign from God.

A few weeks passed. At the end of one long and difficult day I had seen over forty patients. I was drained. The next patient on the list was Jack Ignatius. I remembered him immediately.

'Well, we have the results at hand. There is no hormonal imbalance that is causing you to have difficulty getting erections. Your blood sugar level is fine. I think we should start with medication and see how that goes. You take one tablet about one hour prior to sexual intercourse. You can have side effects. These include headaches and blurred vision. See how you go and let me know.' I wrote out the prescription. He had a couple of questions. I made an appointment to see him again in a few weeks.

A few days later, next patient: Jack Ignatius.

'They don't work, Doc. I tried 'em like you said. Nothin'.

Got the headache, but no stiffy. Is there anything else?' He was wearing a red shirt now. Still the golden jangles.

'Well, that is surprising. Jack, there are several other treatments in our armamentarium. There are pumps that you place over the penis. You pump it up and when the penis engorges with blood you place a rubber band around the base to hold the blood in the penis.' I showed him the device.

'How much does it cost?'

'About five hundred dollars.'

'What else is there? Doesn't sound too romantic, does it?' His face was sleazy.

'Well, there are injections.'

'Injections?'

'You can be taught to inject your penis with a solution that causes it to become erect.'

'Sounds painful.'

'It's not too bad. Lots of my patients use this method. It gives good results.'

'What else?'

I could tell he was not going to inject. 'Well, there is an operation. We can implant a prosthesis into your penis. I have good examples of it here. I showed him the diagrams and went through my 'we have three models' routine. He perked up when I got to the last, the Rolls-Royce of penile pumps.

'How much does this cost?'

'Well, the device alone is about six thousand dollars. Then you have theatre fees, anaesthetic fees and my fees. Are you in a health fund?'

'No, I'll just pay cash, Doc.'

'So you want to go ahead?'

'I like the look of that Rolls-Royce model, Doc.'

Arrangements were made. A couple of weeks later, I had Jack Ignatius's external genitals on show. He was asleep. I noticed his gold chains had been removed.

The operation is a bloody and macabre one. An incision is made below the penis; the penile core is hollowed out with a number of dilators. Then the length is measured with a specially calibrated ruler. The exact size of device is selected. The device is fitted and the scrotum is flayed to allow enough room for the pump to be inserted. Finally, space is made behind the bladder for the reservoir. Once it is all in place, we test it before the final closing stitches are placed.

'What do you think, sister? Good enough?' It was sleazy humour. However, the scrub nurse was always asked whether the erection would satisfy her or not.

Jack Ignatius had a difficult recovery, but he recovered nevertheless. He needed more pain relief than other patients and his wound took a long time to fully heal.

When he came back for follow-up several weeks later, he was healed and was happy with the result. Another satisfied customer, I thought.

About a year later, I had arrived home just in time to watch the news. The leading story was about a paedophilia ring that had been busted by police in Sydney, with links in Thailand. There was Jack Ignatius in handcuffs.

I sat before the television flicking from one station to the other to catch other aspects of the news story. I was horrified. I felt like an accomplice, like turning myself in to the police.

After that, I came to be suspicious of every patient with impotence. The single old man with 'a friend' got a full grilling from me about his sexual proclivities. Thankfully, patients must have complained about me, because I got fewer and fewer referrals for impotence. I didn't mind.

The image of Jack Ignatius with the penile prosthesis I had inserted being dragged away in handcuffs lives with me always. And he was still wearing his gold chains, glittering in the Thailand sun, as he was dragged off to jail.

CHAPTER 15

Shem

I was angry with my friend:
I told my wrath, my wrath did end.
I was angry with my foe:
I told it not, my wrath did grow.

And I watered it in fears,
Night and morning with my tears;
And I sunned it with smiles,
And with soft deceitful wiles.

And it grew both day and night,
Till it bore an apple bright;
And my foe beheld it shine,
And he knew that it was mine,

And into my garden stole,
When the night had veiled the pole:
In the morning glad I see
My foe outstretched beneath the tree.

'A POISON TREE' BY WILLIAM BLAKE

Not too long after Jack began his new life in a Thai prison, I gave up private practice to continue as a salaried doctor. I told my secretary to cancel the rest of my consulting sessions and refer all my patients to the clinic at the hospital that was to become my new consulting rooms.

There was no one on the list to cancel.

As what's called an academic surgeon, I got paid regardless of whether I operated or not. I could then, with conscience intact, advise patients as to what they would need and not what I would want for my own financial survival. I had a title, Senior Lecturer, and I had teaching responsibilities to medical students, albeit only in urology. The title was second rung from the bottom in the university hierarchy, and was a long way from Professor. Nevertheless, it was a title, and with it came a salary. This also meant that I could afford to sub-specialise and decide not to see certain patients. I resolved never to do impotence surgery again.

Freedom came from not being reliant on general practitioners to send me patients. I saw my patients in the outpatients of the hospital. When I decided to do an operation, there was no conflict of interest and payment was not a factor. All the patients were looked after for free by the hospital. For me, this was the ideal way to practise surgery. I love the art and science of my craft, but the business of surgery had not inspired me.

Shem Ehud was an ebullient man. He was only in his forties but in his short life he had seen much death and torture, suffering and fighting; the way people react under extreme fear, the way people's lives can suddenly change in an instant. He had fought in battles, carrying out orders from merciless generals, and he had seen the fear in men's eyes during the last moments of their lives as they realised the wounds he had inflicted upon them were mortal. His wiry, agile frame and determined demeanor gave him away as someone above the ordinary.

Shem Ehud was a retired agent from Mossad, the elite Israeli Army Special Forces.

Yet, today, he was a worried man. He was not in charge. He was facing his own mortality. He was being held hostage, and tortured, by cells that were out of control. He had cancer of the prostate and he had come to me for help.

His referral was '53 M. PSA 19. Otherwise well. Please see and treat'.

I read his referral to him. 'PSA' stood for prostate-specific antigen. A rise in this protein could be measured in the blood and was one of the ways that assisted in screening for prostate cancer.

'I have done some reading, Doc*togh*.' The 'r' in doctor had been replaced with the French guttural sound '*gh*', a sort of clearing of the throat that immediately revealed a person as a Hebrew-speaking Israeli. 'It is above the level it should be. It is likely to be prostate cancer, is it not?'

'Well, it is above the level I would like it to be for your age. Do you have any accompanying symptoms?' I asked, treating him as I would any other patient, despite the difficulty of being faced with the enemy. I, a Muslim of Lebanese origin, could only regard this man as my enemy.

I thought of the times I had sat in the many cafés in Beirut late at night, the laughter of children allowed to stay up late at a family gathering amid the sounds of Fairouz being broadcast though loudspeakers. The distinct smell of the shisha, with its apple-scented tobacco.

Then I thought of the destruction that Israel had wrought on Lebanon. It was indescribable. Twenty-eight members of my family – five below the age of five – were killed during the Israeli annihilation of Lebanon. Six hundred thousand of my countrymen had been made refugees. This man sitting in front of me may have trained the soldiers who continued to rain death and destruction on my country of origin. He could have been indirectly responsible for the disappearance of eight of my extended family in the south of Lebanon. They have never been heard of since. Israel robbed a whole generation of its memories and its spiritual home.

This country, which had always been a peace-abiding trading post (first for the Phoenicians), had seen more than its share of war. It had been invaded and destroyed by the Persians, the Macedonians, the Turks, the French and now the Israelis. The southern city of Tyre – my family home – was the only city in history to resist Alexander the Great. In modern times, it has been the only city to ever resist the Israeli army through the resistance of the Hezbollah. Jesus himself had walked there and in the nearby city of Kana. All was now gone.

I had lost concentration. Ehud was busy answering my questions.

'. . . and occasionally I have troubles passing water, *burghning*. But otherwise, nothing.' He looked up at me.

'Can I ask you a difficult question?'

'Yes, of course,' he said.

'Why did you come to see me? You are, judging from your name and your accent, Israeli. I would guess you were in the army in Israel. Why me?'

'Your reputation, Doc*togh*. That is all, your reputation.' He looked at me with deep blue eyes that reflected the Israeli flag. The flag that symbolically declared the Star of David would rise between the two seas.

'Shem, I will look after you as if you were my brother,' I said with utmost earnestness.

'I believe that you will. Thank you,' he said gratefully. The air had been cleared.

'I will need to feel your prostate. I need you to stand over here, take your pants and underpants down and bend over. I have to examine you through the back passage.' I was a professional. I surprised myself.

'I have not been looking forward to this.' He smiled.

He did as I had told him and I placed a glove on my right hand and lubricated my index finger with KY Jelly. I put my hand gently on his back and inserted my digit into his rectum.

'Do you have family in Lebanon, *Doctogh?*'

I froze. He had read my mind. His bottom tightened around my finger.

'Yes, many, mostly in the south. Some are dead. Some, we do not know whether they are alive or dead,' I said, while feeling a terrible hardness in his prostate, a cancer that spoke to me of eventual death for this Mossad agent. The cancer was still contained in the prostate but only just. However, he was relatively young, and something had to be done. I removed my finger, discarded the soiled glove and washed my hands.

'You can get dressed now, Shem.'

'What did you find?' he asked as he pulled up his pants and buckled his belt.

'I can feel some hardness in the prostate. Coupled with your PSA level, I believe we have no option but to perform biopsies.' I went into my consent patter – you can have a life-threatening infection, you can bleed, you may get pain during urination. He accepted the risk and we went ahead.

A week later, he returned. In front of me was the pathology result: high-grade prostate cancer. His CT scan and bone scan were clear. He had only localised prostate cancer – possibly treatable.

'Well, Shem, it is as you suspected. Prostate cancer. The left lobe of your prostate is fine, but each of the biopsies in the right lobe is involved.' I waited for any reaction. His eyes were watering. *Please do not cry. I cannot cope with emotion today.*

He blew his nose. 'I knew it was going to be bad. I knew it.' He sobbed.

'It could have been much worse, Shem. Your scans are clear. That means the cancer is probably only in your prostate. There are many treatments available. Given your young age and your overall condition, we would certainly try to treat this, aiming for a cure.' The chances were not good, but what other choice did he have?

'I want an operation, *Doctogh*. I do not want radiotherapy. I have read about the side effects of the operation. I can be incontinent and I can lose my potency. But with radiotherapy, I can have all of that and be incontinent of shit as well. I could not live with that.' He was a well-informed patient. I booked him in for surgery.

Three weeks later, a scared Shem Ehud fronted up to my knife. I was probably the only Arab man ever to have approached him with a knife and survived. I made a low midline incision to expose the front of the bladder, then I divided and ligated the dorsal vein complex, dissected the apex of the prostate, cut across the urethra and then lifted the prostate up from in front of the rectum, ligating the numerous arteries and veins that contained between them the nerves that controlled potency. His life and, perhaps more importantly, his sex life depended on my skill. The prostate was removed intact with the seminal vesicles and cancer contained. I had done a brilliant operation, even if I say so myself.

He recovered well, as one would expect. I did ward rounds at least once a day. On day four he had a slight temperature. I prescribed antibiotics. As I wrote in the notes, he reached for his bedside table and showed me a picture of a beautiful young girl.

'She was my daughter.' The word 'was' resonated.

'She was in a bus on her way home from school in Tel Aviv. Someone blew himself up when the bus stopped to pick up passengers. My daughter was leaning out of a window, shouting at her friends. She was torn in two.' He was composed. He had resolved his grief.

'She looks like she would have made a wonderful woman. I am sorry. No cause makes this right.'

'You see, *Doctogh*, they just will not accept that we have a right to exist in peace. They have made our lives like hell. So we have to defend ourselves.' He was trying to convince me.

'Shem, this is a long discussion. You cannot live in peace if the home you occupy belongs to someone else. You came in droves into Palestine in 1948 and took over Palestinian homes and land. Your terrorist organisation wreaked havoc on villages in Palestine, such that you created hundreds of thousands of refugees. Lebanon took them in.

'You have the backing of the US, a country you control.' I was letting loose. I was not going to let him get away with the twisted history that CNN peddles as truth. 'The Middle East crisis is a true David and Goliath story, except the Arabs are a David without a slingshot and you are a Goliath with an army and a military force that is unrivalled. It does not make it right though.'

'But we have a Biblical right to that land,' he said.

'It is a Bible only you believe in. The Palestinians do not believe in your Bible. They have their own. It's called the Koran, and it tells them something different. UN resolutions were passed in 1948 to establish "two" states, Palestine and Israel. Only Israel got established. This is the basic truth of the Middle East. Now it has been made more complex by oil, wealth and geopolitical manoeuvring. Fundamentally, it is a story of a people made homeless by your country.' I had raised my voice. I now regained control of my emotions.

'Anyway, may God bring peace to us all. I accept, Shem, that you have a right to live in peace. Do you accept that the Palestinians have a right to a homeland as well?' I wanted conciliation. I wanted peace with this man.

'Yes, they do. But not at our expense.' He looked up at me from his bed.

I reached out and tapped the back of his hand and smiled. He and I were stubborn men.

A week later, he was back home. He had had an excellent recovery. His pathology showed that I had completely excised his prostate cancer. He was most likely cured.

Six months later, I saw him again for a check-up. His PSA was almost zero and he was continent and starting to have erections. He was very happy and back in control.

'I want to thank you. Really. I know you have treated me well, *Doctogh*. Thank you.' He was genuinely grateful.

He was about to leave but I stopped him. 'There's something I have always wondered, Shem,' I said.

'What is that, *Doctogh*?'

'What is typical Israeli food?' I like food. I had never eaten Israeli food.

'Oh, we have great food. Hummus, tabouli, falafel. My mother makes the best.'

'Listen, Shem,' I said, faking aggression. 'You may have taken our land, mate, but don't take our food too. This is Lebanese food!' We laughed together, shook hands and parted.

We parted not as a doctor and his patient. Not as a Lebanese Muslim and an Israeli soldier. We parted as friends.

CHAPTER 16

Mrs Tobias

Break, break, break,
On thy cold grey stones, O Sea!
And I would that my tongue could utter
The thoughts that arise in me.
O well for the fisherman's boy,
That he shouts with his sister at play!
O well for the sailor lad,
That he sings in his boat on the bay!
And the stately ships go on
To their haven under the hill:
But O for the touch of a vanish'd hand,
And the sound of a voice that is still!
Break, break, break,
At the foot of thy crags, O Sea!
But the tender grace of a day that is dead
Will never come back to me.

'BREAK, BREAK, BREAK' BY SIR ALFRED LORD TENNYSON

She was a beautiful woman, Mrs Tobias. Head held up, high cheekbones, supple neck, she dripped with jewellery. Mr Tobias was a short, unattractive man, and he sat there holding her hand as if he was the patient, as if he was the one with all the pain. I sat opposite them, sentencing her to death.

'I am sorry, Sarah, but despite taking your bladder out . . .'

I wish I had known that your cancer had progressed, as I would never have put you through the torture of taking out your bladder.

'. . . the CT scan result shows that there has been progression of the cancer outside the bladder.'

You are going to die and there is nothing I can do to prevent it.

Silence.

I always wait to see how my words are received.

They both looked at each other with knowing eyes. It is as if you have hold of someone suspended over a cliff; it's the look they would give just as they realise you can't hold on any longer, that you are letting go and they will start their descent – a terrified look where every sinew is attempting to regain or maintain control.

Then, the inevitable question – my most hated question.

'So what does this mean, Doctor?'

What do I say? How can I couch this in terms that do not take away hope but ensure that this person is able to complete the business they need to complete prior to shuffling off their mortal coil?

'Well, Sarah, I believe the cancer is going to keep growing inside of you. There are some experimental treatments available, but you and John need to make a decision about whether or not to let . . . nature take its course.'

Do you understand? I am talking about death here?

'What type of experimental treatments, Doctor?' It was Mr Tobias. Mrs Tobias sat there resigned to the suffering to come. She seemingly understood what I had said clearly and without ambiguity. She had also, in that split second, appreciated she was on a roller-coaster of suffering that had just been erected by her husband's enquiry. It was made out of misguided love, but his love would have been better served allowing nature to take its course. I wasn't telepathic, but after a while you became adept at reading the subtle and not-so-subtle nuances of a patient's facial cues.

'Well . . .' I am staring at Mrs Tobias and the wretchedness that the last three minutes of her life has etched upon her face. She has visibly changed before my eyes, like something from a horror novel in which the handsome young mistress suddenly morphs into an old hag and then to a skeleton. No one else could see it.

'Dr Guise over at oncology has been experimenting with a new chemotherapy regime that is showing some initial benefits.'

Dr Guise puts his research empire first.

Why am I even suggesting this? I am legally bound to offer her all the alternatives, and yet, every logical and ethical thought tells me this is not best for her. She will simply suffer more than she has to.

I look at Mr Tobias. He's in – hook, line and sinker.

'When can we see him?'

You poor fool. Don't do this. Just don't.

'Well, let me see about a referral and let us hear what he has to offer.'

I wrote the torture certificate and gave it to the patient's husband, who was now going to do anything in his power to make sure that his wife did not die. This had become a challenge. When he was working, he used to court challenges, such as making sure no amount of red tape prevented his company from getting a building up on time. He got huge bonuses for cutting through the bullshit and getting the job done. He did not understand, poor fool, that when it comes to human life, the challenge is to understand what the project is in the first place. What lawyers call 'the brief'. Grasping the needs of an individual, understanding those needs and, most importantly, knowing when not to offer medical care, is paradoxically the essence of good medical care. Mr Tobias did not have a clue in this regard.

Two weeks later, Mrs Tobias was no longer Mrs Tobias. Her name was changed to 'Chemotherapeutic trial XAD 45903/298 Subject 597'.

Mr Tobias looked at his wife's new name with glee. He had made this happen in record time. He was 'the Man'. Mrs Tobias was in the bed being pumped full of the latest drugs Dr Guise had received from the pharmaceutical companies. Sarah Tobias looked at me with eyes that said, 'Get me out of here. You know I do not want this.'

'How are you, Mrs Tobias?' I asked, knowing the answer long before the question had a chance to pass through my lips.

'She is doing well,' Mr Tobias interjected. 'Doctor Guise says that the cancer looks like it's responding. He thinks Sarah will be here for another six weeks. She's taking to it well. Her urine bag is functioning although she's not hungry. I've tried to cook her something from home but she's not keen to eat.' Mr Tobias knew it all. He was the managing director now.

Weeks passed. Her cancer kept growing. Dr Guise eventually took XAD 45903/298 Subject 597 off these latest drugs. He sat on the side of the bed and told husband and wife that there was little more that could be done. He felt that she should possibly go home and let nature take its course.

He now had a problem and to solve it Dr Guise simply excluded her from his results and published his paper.

Sarah kept dying.

When I was next called to see Mrs Tobias, she and her husband had just come back from South America, where Mr Tobias had found a doctor who injected cancers with ozone gas and achieved miracle cures. In Sarah's case, he had succeeded in breaching the anterior abdominal wall and the cancer grew out of the lower part of her abdomen like a colourful Indian turban. Reds and browns and yellows – very attractive colours in a dreadful context – death was oozing out and overcoming life.

'I think it did her some good, Doctor, but we had to come back because of the vomiting.' Mr Tobias was still trying. Sarah spoke very little now. Just the occasional deep sigh of resignation.

Inevitably, the dance with hope ceased and one night John held his wife as she looked up and said, 'I love you, John.' His tears streamed down his face onto her forehead. She could feel it no more. She had slipped away.

A few weeks after the funeral, Mr Tobias was left alone with the echoes of his life. He often reached out to hold his wife's hand as he watched television at night, but now it was not there. She had been his reason for living. He felt there was no way to fill the emptiness after her death. The flowers faded, the visits from friends and relatives dwindled, and the ashes sat there silently on the mantle. He was left with a void. In a life-long relationship like John and Sarah's, that void is often impossible to fill.

Each day Mr Tobias walked up the street from the milk bar on the corner, slowly and with no purpose. It was only about half a kilometre, but he tried to make it last as long as possible. He was full of dread for what he had to do next – go home.

He hated home. He looked across to the park opposite. Some mothers had taken their pre-school children for a mid-morning play. The children were screaming as the mothers pushed them on the swings. Despite the noise, they appeared far away. There was a chill in the air and the wind made the cold seem more piercing. He walked past a Chinese restaurant; it used to be their favourite haunt. It was closed. The bistros nearby had attracted most of the customers away and this suburban eating hole could not survive. There was a shabbiness about it now. He remembered the last time he had eaten there with Sarah.

He turned into his driveway and walked across the grass to his front door. He fumbled around in his pockets for the key. This had always driven Sarah mad.

'Why don't you get the key ready before you get there?' she would ask.

He yearned to hear her voice. Instead, all he heard were the echoes of the key as it slowly found its way into the lock. The door opened and he sighed his usual 'I am back' sigh. The 'back to the emptiness of my life' sigh.

Within weeks he had come in to see me. He had a twinge in his lower abdomen and was worried that this could be a cancer. That was how Sarah had been diagnosed: x-rays, CT Scan, blood tests, costs.

Months of, 'Are you sure there is nothing wrong, Doctor?' followed. I came to dread seeing him.

Then, one day, about a year later, John brought his new wife to see me. He bounced into my surgery. She was Filipino, perhaps months older than sixteen. He was sixty.

'Her name is Katrina, Doctor. I – that is, we, are wondering whether it is too late for me to have children?'

CHAPTER 17

Opiated

O Friend! I know not which way I must look
For comfort, being, as I am, opprest,
To think that now our life is only drest
For show; mean handy-work of craftsman, cook,
Or groom! – We must run glittering like a brook
In the open sunshine, or we are unblest:
The wealthiest man among us is the best:
No grandeur now in nature or in book
Delights us. Rapine, avarice, expense,
This is idolatry; and these we adore:
Plain living and high thinking are no more:
The homely beauty of the good old cause
Is gone; our peace, our fearful innocence,
And pure religion breathing household laws.

WRITTEN IN LONDON, SEPTEMBER 1802,
BY WILLIAM WORDSWORTH

Tanya Cordell was a surgeon's wife, and she loved every minute of it. She stood staring at her wardrobe, wondering whether her Bruno Magli black high-heeled shoes or the tan-coloured Prada court shoe would match best with her woven white Chanel suit.

Dr Daniel Cordell had left for work as he usually did at about 5.30 am. He started his day at the Santa Maria Private Hospital doing ward rounds, then drove across town to the Naval Hospital to review the patients he had operated on the day before, and then went to the Victoria Hospital for an early round before going to his rooms for a morning consulting session. Inevitably he worked through lunch.

Sometimes his staff would make him a cheese sandwich that he grabbed on his way to the theatre at one of the four private hospitals to which he was attached and to which he provided an admirable service.

His gross earnings were in excess of a million dollars. Medical insurance cost about $130,000. His car repayments chewed up another $100,000, and then his staff and rooms were in the vicinity of $250,000. This left him with about $500,000 from which a variety of tax-minimising investments in property and shares left him and his wife with about $250,000. They had two children at private schools and owned a yacht and a large mansion, both of which were mortgaged to the hilt.

When they went on holidays, Tanya demanded that they go First Class. He wore Zegna suits and Bruno shoes, his underpants were Calvin Klein and his glasses and pen were Mont Blanc. Last year, his wife had bought him a Philippe Patek watch and told everyone how surprised he was. Appearances were all-important.

He pleaded with his wife to scale back the madness, but his protests went unheard. He had been working now for over 15 years at an average of about 90–120 hours a week and his total net assets were still in the negative. The downturn in the property market and some unwise investments by his financial advisor meant he was rapidly approaching insolvency. He kept this from his wife. She would have been mortified.

At 6 pm his main referring family doctor had rung him with a private patient who needed to be seen because of abdominal pain. He arranged to see her in his rooms that evening. He still had another three hours of work to go and then ward rounds. There were 20 patients waiting in his waiting room. At 7.30 pm he got a phone call from Tanya.

'Have you forgotten about the school concert tonight? Don't tell me I have to go alone AGAIN! You're truly impossible.' She then hung up on him.

He continued seeing patients. He had no choice. He was on a treadmill from which there was no getting off. When he finally got home at 10 pm, his kids were asleep and Tanya was in a frosty mood. He grabbed a beer and a packet of chips and switched the TV on.

'Aren't you going to talk?' she asked sarcastically.

'I just need a break, Tanya.' He had his feet up on the couch and his tie was undone.

'Well, I'm going to book us a holiday. School holidays are coming up and it will be great. The kids are looking forward to it. I spoke with Jenny today from the travel agency and she reckons there's a really divine resort that's just opened up in Bali. Very exclusive and very chic. Just the thing we need.'

He could see she was excited.

'Sarah Mitchell was telling me that she and her husband went there and loved it,' she went on.

Which credit card was he going to use? Not the Amex. That had to be paid at the end of each month, but the others could be stalled. He didn't have the heart to tell her not to even contemplate such foolishness.

She kept on talking, but he could no longer hear her. He fell into a restless sleep. When he woke at 2 am, Tanya had gone to bed and his neck hurt. He got up, went to the toilet, threw his suit on the floor and joined her in bed. She grunted slowly from the disturbance and then rolled over and continued on with her 'Nutcracker Suite' dream, of sugar plum fairies and expensive acquisitions.

The alarm went off almost immediately. It was 5 am. He got up and the next day started.

His descent began innocently. He had back pain and took some codeine. Then one day he prescribed himself some oral narcotics – one or two at first. He was certainly not addicted, he told himself.

Dr Cordell and I shared theatre lists on Wednesday mornings at the Victoria Hospital. He was always dictating notes and trying hard to catch up with stacks of patient records that seemed to emanate endlessly from his Kenneth Cole briefcase.

He couldn't stand academic surgeons so we communicated through a veneer of polite small talk. He would often say in earshot of me, 'Those who can, do, and those who can't, teach!' I despised all he stood for. I refused to think of surgery as a business. It was a calling. I had given up private practice to avoid living his life.

Lately, I had noticed a change in Daniel. He would stretch out between cases and fall asleep in the surgeon's room. He would get cross with nurses and with the theatre staff and his impatience was only getting worse. He seemed to swap into every on-call shift possible and he was often still at work operating when dawn coloured the sky.

'Dan, are you OK?' I asked one day.

'Why the fuck do you ask?' He glared at me.

'Nothing, it's just you are not yourself,' I cautiously replied, taken aback by his vitriol.

The next day in theatre, the nurses were gossiping about Dr Cordell.

'What changes have you noticed?' I asked innocently.

'Everyone can see it. He's totally different. He's become so obnoxious and touchy. He's always complaining about patients not paying bills. God, he must earn enough!' The nurses knew us better than we knew ourselves.

A couple of weeks later I needed to go in at midnight to stem some bladder bleeding in a patient whose tumour I had resected. I walked into the theatre change room and sat down to remove my shoes. I stripped out of my pants and shirt and was looking for theatre scrubs in my size. Someone opened the door behind the row of lockers. I paid no attention. I put on my top and walked around with pants in hand. There, sitting on a wooden bench, was Dr Daniel Cordell with a tourniquet round his arm and a needle plunged deep in his veins. Daniel was shooting up.

'Jesus Christ, Dan. What the fuck are you doing?' I yelled.

He looked up, guiltily at first and then with staunch resolve. 'I've had some terrible back pain, mate. I just need to get it under control to be able to get through tonight,' he said.

'Bullshit, Dan. You have a problem. You need help. We need to get you to see someone,' I said, and sat next to him.

Daniel Cordell looked straight at me. 'You utter a word of this, pal, and you will be taken out. I will fucking make sure you do not see the light of day.' He was threatening in the extreme. Pointing his finger at me, he walked out to operate. It was 2 am. I did not know what to do. I called the hospital operator.

'Get me the Medical Administrator on call please.'

'I don't think we have one. Do you want me to get you the General Manager?'

'Yeah. Anyone will do.' I was panicked.

An endless few moments passed. The chimes of Big Ben reproduced with computer tones entertained me for several minutes.

'Hello.' The voice was sleepy and impatient.

'Are you the Senior Medical Administrator on call today?' I asked.

'Yeah, I think so. What's the problem?' These people were not accustomed to being woken in the middle of the night. I related the incident I had seen a few minutes previously.

'Look, the best thing is to let it go for the moment. Make a report to the Medical Board in the morning. I think that's the cleanest way to handle it. After all, it's your word against his. If you persist, we'll have to get a urine sample from him to test for narcotics. Do you know if there are any missing from the hospital supplies?' He went into management speak.

'I haven't done an inventory. I'm simply reporting the incident and the threat,' I said, exasperated.

'I wouldn't take the threat too seriously.' He wasn't taking it very seriously otherwise he would have to fill out several forms and the hospital would need to pay for security protection for my home. I thought of my kids and wife asleep. I thanked him for his time and hung up. A nurse called me in to operate. Daniel had finished his case and departed. I operated, then sat down to draft a report to the Medical Board, which I faxed from my office at 5 am.

Three weeks later I was called to a hearing of the Board to investigate allegations made against Dr Daniel Cordell. I had a lawyer supplied to me by the Board. Dan sat motionless with his lawyer. My report had been distributed to each of the people on the board. As each question was asked, Dan would consult his lawyer and then give a carefully crafted answer. Reports of several urine tests were made available – all had been clear of narcotics. Dan then made a statement in which he alleged that I had been jealous of his practice and that I had made up these allegations to discredit him.

I struggled to control my anger. It had been a difficult three weeks with whispers in theatres and gossip that was rife. Confidentiality had not been preserved by Administration and each night every noise outside our home made both my wife and I jump. I had slept little.

Daniel was not the only doctor with an addiction, but he was the only one threatening me. Properly controlled, the 14 per cent or so of health professionals that have a substance abuse problem tend to manage their addictions well. Anaesthetists can gather the remnants of vials of narcotics, unused on their patients; nurses might steal morphine destined for a patient in pain from the ward trolley and inject saline in its place; or a resident might buy his hits from the corner drug vendor.

Narcotics are not the only substance abused. For many it is alcohol. With controlled addictions and judicious timing, these addicted doctors function normally and go for years undiscovered; that is, until a patient dies from negligence or their behaviour becomes inappropriate. However, with so many interesting and eclectic characters making up a hospital roster, differentiating between a doctor who is exhausted and one who is narcotised or drunk is difficult. Discerning whether a doctor's over-the-top joviality is due to amphetamines rather than simply a good day can be impossible.

Despite his abuse, I really felt that Dan was more of a threat to himself than to his patients, but there were indicators that informed me he was slowly coming unglued: haphazard entries in the notes; inappropriate rudeness to the ward staff and his trainees; one or two additional complications – but nothing that could stand up in a court of law or at a Medical Board hearing. I wanted him to be helped and to see my whistle-blowing as a means of assistance rather than an attack. This was not the case.

The Board dismissed the threats against me by Dr Daniel Cordell as hearsay. He was asked to undergo random urine testing, which he agreed to do. The following Wednesday, he pushed past me in theatres. Several other surgeons smirked. Daniel was triumphant.

Unjust triumph doesn't usually last.

A month later, Daniel Cordell was called in to operate on a septic abdomen. The theatre staff called for the patient and then started to prepare him for surgery. The anaesthetist placed the lines into the patient, and the nurses counted the swabs and the instruments. All was proceeding normally.

But, unseen by anyone in the theatre complex, Daniel was on the floor of the deserted theatre next door. He placed a tourniquet around his arm and deftly inserted a cannula. He then connected himself to the syringe driver that had injected a measured dose of medication to a patient. He had spotted the leftover drugs and had quietly put the partially used syringes in his pocket. He was looking forward to the high. The heat was off and another urine sample would not be collected for at least another week.

But Daniel had not checked the contents of the syringes he was injecting into his arm. Instead of injecting narcotics to blunt his pain, he had set the syringe driver full of muscular paralysing agent. Both were colourless liquids and both were drawn up in identical syringes by the anaesthetist on the previous case. He knew the difference between them, but Daniel Cordell did not.

As the medication raced through his veins, he felt some twitching of his muscles that he ignored. It then hit him very suddenly. He was having trouble breathing. He was labouring, gasping for air. Instead of the cool dissociation with pain he was expecting, he had an intense discomfort in his muscles as one by one they became paralysed. He tried to reach up to stop the injection, but his arm would not move. He sat in the dark, unable to move his lungs to fill them with air. He was in fact unable to move any of his muscles. It would take him about three minutes to die.

In that time, he would realise what was about to happen to him. His brain would reach blind panic; he would feel his lungs screaming to be allowed to expand. Eventually, he would become unconscious from lack of oxygen, but not before he had time to consider his life, consider his excesses, consider his dishonesty.

Perhaps his last thought was a vision of his wife, Tanya, in the pink Max Mara outfit she had just purchased for their upcoming holiday. His death was as savage and violent as it was silent. His voice was, of course, paralysed too. The diabolical agent that continued to flow into his body made sure that no recovery was possible. No one went into unused theatres in the middle of the night.

No one except Daniel Cordell.

In the theatre next door, the assistant had gone to check the change room, the surgeon's room and the toilet. They rang his home and woke his wife who assured them he had left to go to the hospital at about 1 am. They waited for him in the theatre. Eventually, after an hour or so, the anaesthetist woke up the Head of Surgery and explained the situation.

'We have a patient on the table and the surgeon is nowhere to be found.'

'I'll be right in,' he said. He had no choice.

Daniel Cordell was discovered at 6 am by the morning shift. He was already in rigor mortis. His eyes were open, staring ahead as if looking forward to something better than the hell he had lived. Some said it was suicide. Some blamed me for his death.

Tanya remarried about six months later. The life insurance was very generous. What Daniel was unable to give in life, he had given in death.

CHAPTER 18

To My Wife

I can write no stately poem
As a prelude to my lay;
From a poet to a poem
I would dare to say.
For if of these fallen petals
One to you seem fair,
Love will waft it till it settles
On your hair.
And when wind and winter harden
All the loveless land,
It will whisper of the garden,
You will understand.

'TO MY WIFE WITH A COPY OF
MY POEMS' BY OSCAR WILDE

I met my wife on the first day of medical school. We were students together, residents, and then registrars. We did our examinations a year apart. We both became specialists. She did anaesthesia and I did surgery.

In medical school we only bought one set of texts and we shared. When she did her primaries, I supported. When I did my fellowships, she was there looking after me.

The Chief of Surgery thought he would have a joke by placing us both on the cardiothoracic term as residents working a one in two shift. Hence when she was on call, I was off and vice versa. Our solution was that we did each other's admissions, which gave us a couple of overlapping hours in our schedule. Over Sunday lunch we shared our lives together.

We had a pact with the nurses that unless there was a cardiac arrest, we did not get paged during those precious and rare couple of hours every Sunday. We lived and breathed medicine. We discussed each other's cases. When I was being taught surgery she was being taught anaesthetics. We shared the pressures and the triumphs, the humiliations and the highs. We had done so ever since meeting in medical school.

Very few in the hospital knew of our marriage nor that we had children. It was no great secret, but we felt it was more professional to be discreet about it. Often she would give my anaesthetics and patients would never associate us because her surname and mine were different. Residents who were training with us never suspected us of being together. One resident thought he had the dirt on me when he saw me say farewell to my wife at the airport.

'I saw you yesterday!' he said triumphantly.

'Oh, where?'

'At the airport,' he said, with a knowing air. 'I saw you there with, you know, her.'

'Who?' I played innocent.

'Our anaesthetist. I didn't know you two were an item. How'd you manage it? What if your wife finds out?'

'She is my wife!'

One of the worst things about being married to a doctor is that we often diagnosed each other's ailments. We wouldn't just have a tension headache; it was a brain tumour until proven otherwise. A stomach pain was appendicitis, a bowel cancer or even lymphoma. A leg pain was a sarcoma.

The opposite was also true. Unless we were in intensive care, we would never take a day off. It was a point of pride that during our training and residency neither of us ever had one day off for sickness, until I ended up in intensive care, and then I did need the day off.

On the plane back from a conference in Singapore I developed a migraine. The migraine turned to vomiting. I spewed so much I could hardly get out of the toilet to fasten my seatbelt for landing. No sooner was my belt tightened than I ended up heaving again, only just making it to the airsickness bag. It was then that it hit me. I had a sudden faint feeling, the plane blackening around me.

I put my head between my legs. It was a bad landing so my brace position was probably not out of place. When I sat up, I immediately felt faint again.

Disembarking the plane was next to impossible. I could hardly make it a few metres without having to sit down. At passport control the officer didn't make sense to me. I was surprised they allowed me back in the country – they must have suspected drug or alcohol abuse.

Eventually, I was able to retrieve my baggage and make it out. Thankfully, my wife was waiting.

'I can hardly stand up,' I said. 'I feel really faint.' I was short of breath, I needed to sit down again.

'God. Stop it. You just want to avoid drinks with the neighbours.' She had no pity.

'No, really. I am absolutely sick.' I wanted to spew again.

'Well, I'll get you home. You can sleep it off. Have you been drinking?' She knew I did not drink, but I must have looked punch-drunk.

'Stop somewhere, I need to spew.' After a very public roadside retch, I made it home only by lying down in the car, reclining the front seat completely. I felt like there was a flock of birds in my chest.

'I think I have atrial fibrillation. Take my pulse,' I demanded. Atrial fibrillation is a condition where a part of the heart beats uncontrollably and transmits electrical signals to the rest of the heart such that the pulse rate goes up significantly. Despite that, the cardiac output is diminished. It can occur spontaneously. It can also be caused by a myocardial infarction, a heart attack.

She took my pulse. 'Yeah, you do. Maybe it's all the vomiting.'

'I need to lie down.' I felt deathly sick by now. I wanted to sleep. My wife went out to drinks, ignoring the sinister possibility that my atrial fibrillation was due to anything other than a spontaneous physiological cause and that it would pass with rest.

I woke later in the afternoon.

'How are you now?' She was waiting for me to wake up.

'A bit better. But I still have this strange feeling in my chest. Take my pulse again.'

'Do you think you are well enough to move the bookcase to the study?' She and I were trying to ignore the whole illness. My heart beating abnormally could not possibly be due to a myocardial infarction, a terminal viral myocarditis, an aortic dissection. The desire that it was nothing was our overwhelming need; it made us ignore any possibility that it could be serious.

'You know what? I think you need bananas!' my wife announced.

'Bananas? Why?' I was surprised by this suggestion.

'Well, with all the vomiting you have probably lost quite a bit of potassium. You need potassium and there are thirty millimoles of it in every banana.' She was always full of useful information.

'So . . . I would need to eat at least three of them.' Ninety millimoles was a standard dose.

'Here, three bananas.' We waited about half an hour, chatting on the bed. Perhaps it was the bananas, or perhaps it was the rest, but I felt a lot better. However, I still had an abnormally beating heart.

I got up and soon we were moving the bookcase. I was still breathless and had to sit down every metre or so, but we shifted it.

'My pulse is still really abnormal. It's so strange.' I was analysing the symptom.

'It could be a mitral rupture? Maybe it is a dissecting aneurysm and you're about to die?' We both laughed at that suggestion.

We see so much pain, so much disease. But it is always someone else's.

By late evening, I was feeling uncomfortable again. I decided to ring a friend who is a physician. I explained the abnormal pulse and the fact that I was feeling better now. I explained the bananas and the possible link with potassium.

Rob advised hospitalisation, but I talked him out of it. His wife was an anaesthetic colleague of my wife. She rang back.

'I do not want to speak with you,' she said in an assertive tone, 'I want to speak with your wife.' My wife picked up the phone and put it on speaker.

'If you had a 38-year-old patient in hospital with his first bout of atrial fibrillation, would you give him three bananas as therapy and send him home?'

The question shocked us into reality. Here I was with a condition that could portend a host of very serious and life-threatening conditions and yet we had glibly ignored all the symptoms, hoping the whole thing would go away.

The late shift was on in the casualty department.

'I just need to have a set of electrolytes done,' I told the resident on call. This would analyse whether my abnormal cardiac rhythm was due to an imbalance of sodium and potassium brought about by me vomiting. These electrolytes are vital for cell function and even minor fluctuations can result in profound physiological effects.

'Sure, sir.' He was not going to argue with a senior colleague. One fringe benefit of going to hospital as a practitioner was that you could jump the queue, walk through the plastic doors labelled 'NO ENTRY'. You were 'one of us' and not 'one of them'.

The charge sister was a crusty nurse from the old school. She was not standing for any nonsense. 'Are you here as a doctor or are you here as a patient?' She was looking straight at me as I stood in the middle of the doctor's room with a tourniquet on my arm and the resident halfway through taking blood. He jumped so much he missed the vein and had to try again.

'I suppose I am here as a patient,' I said.

'Well, then. You get into that gown and you lie down on that bed over there. NOW.' She was a tough nut.

Before long, I had monitors attached to me. Faces went pale when they looked up to see my pulse racing at 170 beats per minute. I was in trouble. Just out of earshot, one doctor told my wife it was amazing I was still conscious. I was now a patient. No longer was I one of them; I was someone with something wrong. The cognitive dissonance was impossible to handle.

'We'll need to get you to cardiac intensive care. You may have had an infarct. This could be serious.' The cardiology resident was trying to be reassuring.

'Fine,' I said. 'I just wanted it fixed in time for my operating list tomorrow.'

'I really think you'll need to cancel the list, sir.'

It suddenly dawned on me that everyone thought that whatever I had was serious.

'We may need to defibrillate you.' This was said very carefully and slowly so that I understood the implications. Electricity was passed through the heart through electric paddles. Most of the time, this restarted normal rhythm in the heart. However, in doing so, a clot is sometimes dislodged from the heart and ends up in the brain – a career-stopper for a surgeon.

I really did not want this. The night resident came to do an admission into cardiac intensive care. A more substandard medical examination had rarely been seen at the Victoria Hospital. He was too overwhelmed to put his stethoscope on my chest or feel my abdomen. He did not ask whether I had travelled recently or whether I had been exposed to any viral illnesses.

'There's nothing wrong with your abdomen, is there, sir?' he asked. I guess he felt I had a better grasp of my own condition. 'I assume you're otherwise well, sir? There's no need to feel your tummy.'

He was doing me a favour in his eyes. What he was actually doing was delivering terrible healthcare because I was a senior colleague. His intention was to protect me from the discomfort of a junior examining someone senior to him. The reality was that he was endangering my life.

Had he examined me properly, he would have found no cause for my atrial fibrillation. In fact, I was healthy. This was nothing but an oddity of the heart's rhythm that needed time to resolve. It had probably been caused by my intense vomiting on the plane.

By the next morning, my heart was back to normal. It had reverted to a normal rhythm as quickly as the abnormal one had appeared in the first place. I sat in a room in cardiac intensive care, surrounded by the other patients, many of whom were in their eighties and who would probably never make it out alive. Lunch was served. Steak and chips, but with no salt.

Some misguided dietician somewhere in the hospital had no doubt read articles about the slight elevation to blood pressure that was possible through excessive salt intake. She had obviously skipped the articles about undigested red meat build-up in the lower intestine or about artery-loving fried potatoes.

Some of the patients had been taken to exercise. I read an article once claiming that for every hour of exercise you do as a young person you add an hour to the end of your life. I gave up exercise that day. Imagine giving up valuable and healthy hours in your youth pumping iron at the gym, running imaginary distances on the treadmill, in exchange for hours in your old age when there was a good chance every day would be a prayer for death. Imagine trading time as a youth for time as an old man. This was not for me.

I laugh at adverts that say 'Smoking Kills!' Has no one told the anti-smoking lobby that 'LIFE KILLS!' Tally up the causes of death for the clean-living, non-smoking, daily-exercising freaks that pound the pavements of life and frown at me sitting in the sun having a smoke and the causes of death add up to 100 per cent. We all die, not just the smokers. There is a quest for immortality today, which is no less misguided than the embalming of the pharaohs or the virgin sacrifices of the Incas.

It all comes down to quality of life, not length. Change the adverts to say, 'If you exercise you will have a better sex life', or 'You will not struggle walking up a hill', and maybe more people might exercise. Tell the smokers that their breath stinks when they kiss: it's more likely to make them quit smoking than gory pictures of amputated, gangrenous limbs. Those adverts and the knowledge of impending doom from smoking never seemed to work for me.

Perhaps it was the nicotine deprivation or a sudden dissatisfaction with an underwhelming healthcare experience, but I insisted on getting salt to put on my chips.

The nurse was quite distressed that a patient in cardiac intensive care would ask for table salt. I think she would have been more able to cope had I asked for a cigarette.

'I'll get the dietician to come and speak with you.'

'If I do not get salt to put on these chips within the next minute, I will be taking these wires off my chest and leaving this hospital. I want salt on my chips and I want it now!' I was really quite irrational at this point.

Multiple nurses appeared, as well as the orderlies. This was the standard response to patients who were irrational – sedate or tie them down.

'I want salt. Get me the dietician.'

'Just calm down, Doctor. We will try and get some salt.'

I was already disconnecting myself from the monitors. I put my slippers on and walked off to the nurse's tea-room, which I knew would have salt. There it was in the middle of the table. The Saxa salt shaker. I grabbed it and walked back to my bed. I now had an entourage of several orderlies and two nurses trailing me. I stood over my chips and poured an excessive amount of salt on them.

I sat down, put a fork through the first of many chips, and ate them in full defiance of the rules that were laid down by autocratic healthcare workers who probably had never had to endure unsalted chips.

I looked around at the other patients, who by now were salivating for the salt that was piled in mounds on my chips. They had no idea how to manipulate the health system to ensure their care was comfortable or even met their needs as individuals. Their beds were made sporadically. They did not know that beds should be made daily and that there is a complaint mechanism to ensure that they got good care. Their rooms should have been cleaned. However, they did not know that, and when the cleaner did not appear for days it was not a noteworthy event.

Food that was unpalatable, a lack of cleanliness and an overwhelming untidiness were now the hallmark of many hospitals. When I had been a resident, the cleaner for a ward was employed by the ward. There was single-point accountability. The charge sister of the ward inspected each room and bathroom. Woe betide the cleaner who had missed soiling on one of the tiles. Woe betide the nurse whose patients had unmade beds.

Over the past few years, outsourcing had become the norm. Massive cleaning companies were given contracts to ensure that the hospital was cleaned. This translated to a lack of single-point accountability. The reporting lines for cleaners were now outside the normal hospital hierarchy. If you were dissatisfied with the cleaning on a ward, you rang an office in town. You were not in a position to fire the incompetent or lazy cleaner who had actually done the cleaning on your ward. For the companies, the less it cost to clean the hospital the more profits they made. So, there was a constant pressure to do less. Instead of daily cleaning, it was the norm to clean a room only once the patient was discharged. Hence, if the patient was in hospital for a few weeks it was not uncommon to see a filthy room with dirt piled under the bed.

I felt so sorry for the patients around me who were not armed with the knowledge to influence their passage through the health system. I knew the number to call to get maintenance to grease the squeaky door to my hospital room that kept me awake at night. I knew the supervisor to call to ensure that my bathroom was kept clean. I knew how to ask questions about my care that ensured I received the best specialists and the best advice. The patients around me on that ward did not know. They took what they were given in a rationed and under-resourced health system that barely served their needs.

I felt suddenly ashamed to be a part of this health system.

CHAPTER 19

Julia

Lady, the sun's light to our eyes is dear,
And fair the tranquil reaches of the sea,
And flowery earth in May, and bounding waters;
And so right many fair things I might praise;
Yet nothing is so radiant and so fair
As for souls childless, with desire sore-smitten,
To see the light of babes about the house.

EURIPIDES

A woman who wants children and cannot have them is a terrible sight. There is a pitiful look in her face that speaks of a great yearning. A deep hunger. A struggle for survival. It is often said that it is the male who is desperate for his progeny to continue, for his genetics to be passed on. However, in my experience, it has always been the female pushing, exploring every avenue, demanding every treatment, subjecting herself and her husband to the most enormously torturous measures in order to become pregnant.

Every miscarriage is a deeply felt grief. Sex becomes a mechanical and ritualistic chore to be timed for most effect, to coincide with the ideal circumstances for sperm to fertilise the tiny ovum. Each month, the anxious wait and then the disappointment of a period. The awful false hope of a late period.

Julia was desperately in love with her husband, Walter. They had met at university and had been together ever since. He was an accountant and she was a financier. She was very successful in her career. He was infertile.

He had been referred to me as a last-ditch effort to see if we could harvest sperm from his testes so that the sperm could be implanted into Julia's harvested eggs in vitro. I had little hope that this would work. His blood tests showed a level of follicle-stimulating hormone (FSH) that was over three times the normal figure. FSH is suppressed in males when spermatozoa are produced in the testes. When no sperm can be produced, the FSH is not suppressed, and this can be measured by a blood test.

I explained the side effects of harvesting the sperm by testicular biopsy.

'Finally, you could lose your testes, although there is very little chance. Do you have any questions?' I finished my long, pre-rehearsed consent speech.

'How soon can it be done?' she asked, the wild animal desperate for survival of her genes. No consideration for the pain or risk to her husband's testicles.

'Next week?'

Arrangements were made.

Testicular biopsies for infertility were a major disruption to the orderly running of theatres. A pathology assistant was brought into theatres and stood by with a large number of jars to collect the biopsies, microscope and various solutions to preserve the live sperm in liquid nitrogen. The first task was to examine the specimen to ensure that there were sperm in the biopsy.

Walter was brought in on the trolley.

'Are you all right, Walter?' I asked reassuringly.

'Fine, Doctor. How soon do I get the result?'

'It will take us a couple of days to get the samples analysed, Walter. I will make an appointment for you and Julia for Thursday. Is that okay?'

The result is known immediately; however, I hated a scene in theatre. The last time I told someone there was no sperm found on the biopsy, I had to call a psychologist to counsel them and it delayed subsequent cases by hours.

The biopsy is done under local anaesthetic. I brought Walter's gown up and his penis and testicles were exposed. Everyone in the theatre went on with his or her business. Nowhere is nudity better tolerated than in the operating theatre. Occasionally, a penis is remarkable: for example, when it is grossly injured or has ballooned into the occasional embarrassing erection. Otherwise, it might as well be the forearm that has been exposed.

I scrubbed and came in dressed for surgery. I prepared Walter's skin with Betadine solution – this killed the vast majority of bacteria – and covered him with sterile drapes, leaving only his external genitals exposed.

I looked across at the laboratory technician and asked if he was ready.

'Just give me a minute,' he replied. The specimen had to be very fresh. 'Okay, go ahead.'

I grabbed Walter's testicle between my thumb and forefinger. He winced. I had to be firm otherwise the testes might slip during the biopsy. I took the syringe of local anaesthetic from the nurse and injected it into the skin to form a large bleb. He winced again. This was a painful part of the procedure and the quicker it was over, the better.

'Scalpel.'

The dull blue scalpel was placed firmly in my hand. It used to be shiny steel but disposable blue scalpels were more cost-effective.

I stabbed deeply into the testicle where the local anaesthetic had been administered. Tan-coloured testicular material oozed out as I squeezed the testes.

'Scissors.'

Scissors were put into my hand. I cut the material that had oozed out and put scissors and material into the first jar that was now held out to me by the nurse. This was passed to the technician.

'Stitch.'

Still holding the testes with my left hand, I passed a chromic stitch through from one side of the wound to the other and then tied the knot. The nurse cut the stitch. My part was done. The technician was now doing his part. A third of the biopsy is frozen, another is placed in solution and the last is used fresh for examination under the microscope. As Walter was being rolled out on his trolley, the technician whispered to me, 'Nothing.' He could see no sperm in the sample.

Three days later, I had to break the news to Julia and Walter. She was devastated. He was calm; he talked about adoption. She shot a fiery look towards him.

'Would you really be happy with adoption?' she asked huskily.

'There are lots of kids out there who need a home, love, care. Why not? It doesn't have to be my biological make-up. I think I could love them regardless.'

They left resolved to adopt. Months of form-filling, interviews and waiting followed. The adoption authorities had a duty of care to perform adequate due diligence on the new couple to ensure they were desirable parents. This often resulted in frustration from the impatient couples awaiting the child they craved.

Finally the call came through: Julia and Walter had picked up the child, a gorgeous young boy of about six weeks, born to a drug-addicted mother who could barely cope with herself, let alone the concept of having a child to rear.

Two years later they were granted another child. Jacob and Sarah grew up in a loving and nurturing home. Julia and Walter's love for each other remained strong, and Julia cherished her role as a mother with great vigour. There was never a mention that the children were adopted. Her career grew stronger and they decided that Walter would devote more of his time to looking after the children. He got them to school each day and did homework in the afternoon with them. He was a model father.

I saw him a couple of times in my university rooms for various lower urinary tract symptoms – minor in the most part. Each time he described a happy and well-adjusted family enjoying nurturing the wonderful children that were theirs emotionally if not biologically.

One day, I looked down at my appointment list to see Julia's name. There was no referral. She had made an appointment to see me and the secretary noted on the file 'Private Matter . . . she would not tell me what it was about!'

'Can I speak to you in absolute confidence, Doctor?' She looked anxious and perturbed.

As part of her job, Julia had to travel a lot. On one such trip, she was the keynote speaker for a conference and was awarded a medal by her profession. The president of the conference was a suave single man in his early forties. One thing led to another, and Julia, although still in love with Walter, slept with this man. She told me it had been great sex. He made her orgasm like she had never orgasmed before. This man knew parts of her body that even she did not realise existed.

She'd left his room at dawn, avoided him at the farewell session and averted her eyes from his at the check-out. He got the message – she was overwhelmed with guilt. He had seen it before with other married conquests. He thought he might give her a call at the office in the next couple of weeks, but he forgot.

She arrived home, and life went on as normal.

Three weeks later, her period did not arrive. She waited a couple of days but nothing happened except that she could feel her breasts slightly enlarge. She did not need the results of the pregnancy test to tell her what she knew. Julia was devastated. She had spent weeks in anguish. Walter was a jealous man. If she told him, there was no question he would leave her. If she had the baby, he would immediately know.

What to do? She sat at dinner staring at her adopted children and her husband, carrying her own child within her; the one thing that she had always needed to make her a complete woman.

'How dangerous is an abortion?' She was quite determined.

'Julia. Surely Walter will understand. It is only a mistake. It does not influence his love for you. Do you not think that being honest with him is going to be the best way?' The unborn child was hers biologically. This was the very event this lady had waited for all her life. How could she deny herself this fulfilment?

'But it's NOT Walter's child. He'll never understand.'

There was nothing I could say or do to dissuade her. I referred her to a colleague who I hoped might help her make a better decision.

A week later, she was sobbing inconsolably as the suction tubing invaded her uterus and, bit by bit, evacuated her baby. Julia felt her soul being sucked out of her.

CHAPTER 20

My Mother

If I had thought thou couldst have died,
I might not weep for thee;
But I forgot, when by thy side,
That thou couldst mortal be;
It never through my mind had past
The time would e'er be over
When I on thee should look my last,
And thou shouldst smile no more.

'IF I HAD THOUGHT THOU COULDST
HAVE DIED' BY CHARLES WOLFE

Years passed with patients, practice, promotions and my growth of confidence as a surgeon. My research as well as my contributions to various large projects in education earned me the ultimate accolade – the title of all titles for an academic – I was promoted to the position of Professor of Surgery. This gave me immense political credibility, my own department, and meant I was able to shape the educational programs for the undergraduates.

My two sons were growing up well. My dreams had come true.

The most satisfying part of my professional role was guiding and mentoring residents. I would see them coming in as medical students, and I had now been in surgery long enough to see some of them as registrars. I helped them with exams and with life. They had the same fears, emotions, fatigue and desperation that I had had as a resident. I tried to make their journey easier. 'It will be OK.' 'This is how to answer your examiners in the *viva voce*.'

I taught them the five aphorisms I had developed as a surgical registrar years before.

'For you to be my resident and to be good at your job, these are the "Five rules of Khadra". Learn them well and live by them and we will all get on:

Rule number one: Meticulous attention to detail. (Interpretation: patients die because we do not pay attention to detail.)

Rule number two: Never assume. (Interpretation: if you order a test, never assume the test was done. If you send a patient for an x-ray, never assume it was OK because no one bothered to contact you to tell you there was a fracture after all.)

Rule number three: There is only one exception to rule number two. Always assume the worst. (Interpretation:

a gut ache is always a burst aortic aneurysm until proven otherwise.)

Rule number four: Your job is to make me look good. (Interpretation: we are a unified team with me at the head. Your poor work reflects badly on the team and hence on me. Make no mistakes because that makes me look bad.)

Rule number five: The rule of survival is 'Eat, sleep and piss at every opportunity'. (Interpretation: self-evident.)'

But this time I was not teaching. I was not mentoring. I was watching.

An eager resident stood listening to the patient's chest. He could hear the loud murmur from a heart weary of beating, a heart that had endured much and was now ready to stop. The patient was breathing with that awful sighing that is typical of impending death. I sat on a chair in the corner, wondering what the resident was planning to do. Out of his pocket came a torch. With his left hand he prised open the patient's closed eyes and shone the torch into the window of the soul, looking for life. The pupils reacted and the patient winced.

Next, he pulled back the gown to uncover her scarred and wasted abdomen and commenced examining the various organs therein contained. Liver, spleen, bowels. He looked ponderously and appeared wise – facial expressions taught to all doctors throughout their training. Never reveal your thoughts or uncertainty. Always look wise.

The patient was a 60-year-old woman with terminal scleroderma, a disease where the body decides that the skin, the lungs, the oesophagus, the kidneys and the joints are foreign and hence have to be destroyed. She had spent 20 years battling the disease that had started when she was in the prime of her beauty and her joy.

It started with a small callous on the back of her hand. A couple of years later, some pain in her wrists and then the deformity of her knuckles. Gradually it had progressed to an inability to swallow, as her oesophagus was slowly destroyed.

Eventually, the skin of her face was pulled tight with inflammation, giving her a corpse-like appearance. Several years previously a tube had been inserted into her abdomen to help her feed and a small, motorised pump on a stand was her constant companion. In the last two years she was unable to bathe herself, wipe herself, feed herself or dress herself. Her husband did all this. My father.

The resident looked up at me. 'I think she has an infection and we should take blood cultures and start her on antibiotics. Is she your mother, sir?'

'Yes, she is,' I said.

'I loved your talk about the future of surgery last month, Prof. It was really inspirational.' He had recognised me from the keynote address I had given at the College of Surgeons the month previously. He was working on his career now. This young man had ambitions of becoming a surgeon and he knew that I held power to stop his progress or to help him on his way. Treating my mother was a big break for him – an opportunity to impress. I had morphed into the bosses that had influenced me in my training.

However, nothing mattered to me but the woman now on the bed, from whose womb I had been born. He had not lived with this woman. He had not seen her constant pain – her prayers for death. He had not sat with my father as he unblocked her tube in the middle of the night. He had not endured the sheer helplessness of a surgeon who could operate on the most advanced of cancers, who could cure the incurable, and yet could do nothing for his own mother.

This woman had survived migration. This woman had sacrificed all she had to feed, clothe and educate her only son. I will never forget what she did for me.

My mother had little in the way of formal schooling and despite this had educated herself by completing various correspondence courses. She had taught me about poetry and classical music and had created a career for herself as a healthcare interpreter. She sat for hours with me as I did my homework and guided and motivated me. She sat at the back of the auditorium when I won my first public-speaking competition and at every speech day and school concert. This woman had saved every dollar she earnt, only to spend it on me.

When there was a textbook to buy for my schooling, it was bought. When my father came home from his day as a factory worker, smelling of grease and oil, she washed his clothes separately so that mine did not smell. This woman had ensured that I ate only the freshest apples and the ripest fruit, and that she and my father ate the leftovers. On the day of my graduation she had worn the newest dress she owned, bright floral polyester with patches artfully embroidered into the flower stems. Her pleasures and her needs had been put aside for the welfare of her son, whose future she was determined to secure.

This young resident had never known the pain of being poor. He had never known what it was like to go to the beach but have no ability to buy an ice cream. He saw me driving my BMW but had no vision of the 22-year-old Morris Minor in which my mother had driven me around.

Now this boy was trying to impress me by suggesting he start treatment to help elongate a life that had long been terminated. He had the mistaken belief of modern health care ingrained in his training and his outlook, that length of life beats quality of life – every time. Save the patient at all costs.

'I do not think that's a good idea,' I said wearily.

'But, Prof, she may have a simple infection that could be easily treated. We must give her antibiotics. We should also do a full blood count and electrolytes. This could be reversible.' He was anxious to ensure that all bases were covered. He was confused by my assertion that his excellent medical suggestions were not correct. 'Your mother's breathing is worrisome. I don't know whether she's snoring or has pneumonia. I can't wake her up.' He was matter-of-fact. He assumed this was another turn in her long illness. He did not have enough sense to realise that her breathing was actually Cheyne Stokes breathing, a portend of inevitable death.

I had passed the night before next to her bed at my parents' home. My father had called around midnight. He had spent half of the last twenty years waiting in emergency rooms in various hospitals while my mother was scoped, prodded, blood-let, x-rayed and admitted to stabilise her condition. Then she would be sent home to live again. A living death.

I arrived that night to find that she had soiled herself and wet the bed. She was grunting with every breath. I contemplated doing nothing for a long time and then at 5 am I called the ambulance. She needed to be nursed and my father and I could not care for her any longer.

When the doctor had said, three years earlier, that my

mother needed to have a tube inserted into her abdomen, my parents did not even contemplate disagreement. They, like so many dealing with chronic illness, knew no better. When the doctor said she needed every joint in both hands replaced, they did not consider asking 'Why?' When the hospital had arranged physiotherapy to help improve her walking they went along every Thursday. When the dietician had recommended high-calorie feeds, my parents sacrificed more of their meagre pension to purchase the sickening fluid that was meant to add weight to my mother's wasted frame. The triumphs of modern healthcare were not serving my mother.

I had, to this point, not interfered with her care. I left her to be looked after by doctors I trusted and a system that was, for me, life itself. No more. This system had to be manipulated and used now. One could not stand back and take all it offered without question. I had had an inkling of this when my heart had gone into a funny rhythm and I had ended up in coronary care. Now I needed to take control, completely and absolutely.

Question the care. Commit treason.

'Look,' I said to the eager resident. 'She has really suffered a lot. I think we would prefer that you keep her comfortable and let nature take its course. We have been through this before. The last thing she needs now is even more treatment, tests, suffering. She has Cheyne-Stokes respiration and at the very least she has suffered a major brain event. Antibiotics are not going to be helpful.' It was now my turn to show my mother love.

In my mind it could never be seen as a loving gesture, a pure act of care and prudence, to allow the mindless machinery of modern medicine to absorb her into its cogs and spit her out again, alive, and back to her dismally protracted life.

'I will need to discuss this with the physician on call today,' I said. The resident was confused and concerned. He disappeared to make phone calls.

I looked up at my mother. Thoughts of our life together came flooding into my mind. We often had long chats about my life, my dreams, and my ambitions. I would relate to her the tribulations of each day. There was not a day in which I did not phone her or visit.

I remembered the last time I had seen her truly happy and free of pain. It was a lifetime ago when we had celebrated the sheer joy of reading the letter from the university together:

'It is with great pleasure that I inform you that you have been accepted on a course leading to the degree of Bachelor of Medicine . . .'

I remembered her dancing around the lounge room.

'My son is going to be a doctor. A famous doctor. A surgeon.'

I had not understood the logic or the motivation of sacrifice for the ones you love. I had not understood that there was happiness and a joy in doing without so that your child can have the best until I'd had children of my own. Their birth turned the guilt that had haunted me throughout my youth to an understanding of the joy of sacrifice.

Her arthritic hands had held on to the bottle of milk tightly as she fed my newborn sons. That was the only other time I had seen pure joy on her face. Joy and pride flashed like lightning in an otherwise dark life.

I now watched her breathe. She was experiencing that deep unconscious anxiety that comes just before death is imminent. I contemplated getting the nurse to give my mother Valium or some morphine to alleviate her anxiety. It was not necessary.

I looked up at my mother, whose breathing had changed character.

I stood up close to the bed.

The resident returned. 'I've spoken with Prof. He feels that we should go ahead with antibiotics.' He stopped talking. He could see that it was too late even for his infallible treatments.

My mother was taking her last breaths now. Her lungs were not clearing air. I watched her neck, looking for her carotid pulse. She was breathing no more. A long minute and then the pulse stopped. My mother had died.

I leaned down to her face and kissed it. I whispered in her right ear, 'There is no God but one God and Mohammad is his Prophet.' I walked around the bed and did the same in her left ear.

These were our beliefs and I wanted her to die in peace.

As I stood over her body as it began the process of rejoining the dust from whence it came, I immediately began to miss her.

'Oh, for the touch of a hand that is gone and the sound of a voice that is still.'

My father came in shortly afterwards and tears streamed down our faces. We hugged, knowing that we were on our own now, without her guiding hand.

*

Over the last few years I had tried to present each patient with dispassionate options. These are the risks of doing the operation. These are the risks of doing nothing. This will be the consequence of doing nothing. Your loved one will continue at home for a period until the renal cancer spreads. When it spreads it will probably spread to the bones first and then the lungs. Inevitably, death will come.

Recognising when it was right *not* to offer care was the hardest decision that a surgeon ever faced. Knowing when not to operate was a much harder decision than knowing when to operate. Anyone could be trained to do the mechanical, the techniques that would result in a kidney being removed or a prostate being taken without the nerves being injured. A well-trained butcher is capable of the techniques. We are trained so that we know how to make these decisions in the interests of our patients.

It was laughable to me how long a bank took to approve a loan, or how long it took a venture capitalist running an investment fund to make a decision of investment. Meanwhile, surgeons make decisions that affect life and death, quality of life, others' futures, every single day. Here is true bravery. Making a call of which the ramifications were life itself. That is what we do. No more and no less. How many medicolegal lawyers are capable of making such decisions? How many politicians sitting in judgement of surgical training and attempting to usurp control from the various Colleges have the spine that even our junior residents exhibit on a daily basis?

At my mother's funeral, the priest read the prayer of the dead. I cried as her grave was being filled with dirt and I felt my hands being pressed gently. I looked down to see that my two boys – my six- and seven-year-old sons – had moved quietly ahead of the assembly to stand by my side at the grave. They, with their tiny hands, did more to comfort me than all the words that were offered that day.

And so the generations continue, in life, and in surgery.

CHAPTER 21

The Sick Rose

O Rose, thou art sick!
The invisible worm,
That flies in the night,
In the howling storm,
Has found out thy bed
Of crimson joy;
And his dark secret love
Does thy life destroy.

'THE SICK ROSE' BY WILLIAM BLAKE

Jo Tavali was 22 and beautiful. Dark hair and eyes of blue with slightly tanned natural skin that was flawless, and a body with not an ounce of fat. The clothes that adorned it had been picked for fashion and not for comfort. Jo lived with Mrs Tavali, the mother, in a small flat provided by the government and surrounded by graffiti, gangs and fast exits from crime scenes. It was not uncommon for the ambulance to be scraping someone up from their block of flats. Gunshots, old people dying alone and forgotten for days, stabbings – all were common occurrences.

The police knew the housing-commission establishment well. Jo's father was serving time for attempted murder. He had bashed his wife to the point of death twice. Jo was relieved the old man was in jail. Jo was now able to take good care of Mrs Tavali. Whatever the unpleasantness, it could be forgotten as soon as they stepped into the flat and closed the door.

They had painted it beautifully and kept it immaculately tidy and clean. They always had fresh flowers in vases, a spread on the sofa that was a shade of orange and that matched the lime-green seats around the glass dining-room table. Jo's room was a picture, in pinks, roses and lilacs, and it had a dressing table with a large assortment of perfumes, stockings and panties with lace and dresses for every occasion.

The only problem was that Jo was a boy and not a girl.

Now he was staring at a gush of blood emanating from his penis into the toilet and he felt faint. He could not take the sight of blood. He sat down on the bowl and looked between his thighs. Definitely red, must be blood. He shouted to his mum. She called the ambulance and within an hour he was in hospital.

When my registrar called me to see Jo, there was levity in his voice.

'I have a young man, er . . . woman . . .who's had significant hematuria [blood in the urine] today. His haemoglobin is normal and his blood pressure and pulse rate are uncompromised.'

'Have you done any imaging?' I asked.

'No. Not yet. What would you suggest?' He was only in his first year and he had a lot to learn.

'Get a CT scan and get him to come to my rooms with it later this afternoon.' I hung up. Dealing with hematuria was something this trainee should already know.

Jo was my last patient for the day. Joshua David Tavali. He was dressed in a chiffon dress with high-heeled courts. His stockings had tiny pink roses on a black background. I did a double-take myself regarding whether he was a male or female.

No trauma, no infections. HIV status last checked two months ago: clear.

So what could cause blood in this man's urine?

I opened the envelope containing the CT scan. There, larger than life, was a 10-centimetre renal tumour hanging off his right kidney; patches of dark and light, irregular outline, no venous invasion. I was not expecting a tumour, not at his age. I had thought he might have a stone, but not a tumour.

I looked up at Jo. I did not want to tell him my findings yet.

'Jo, I need to examine you. Would you take your dress off and strip down to your undies, ummm . . . I mean your panties. I'll be right over once you are ready.'

I stood staring out of the window, waiting. There was a mother trying to keep a three-year-old boy from killing himself by running across the street. He was screaming.

'Readddyyyyy,' announced the feminine lilting voice behind me. I turned to see Jo fully naked, lying back on the bed, hands above his head.

I grabbed for a towel and placed it delicately on his genitals. I started examining his abdomen: liver, spleen, bowels, left kidney and then finally the right kidney. The mass was palpable through the skin. This was going to be some operation. A large vascular tumour. At least he was thin, which would make things easier.

'I will also need to examine you below,' I said, somewhat uncomfortably. I removed the towel and examined his scrotum. Jo had smaller testicles than normal. His penis was becoming erect with the manipulation of my examination. It is not uncommon for males, not only gay males, to get an erection while being examined. It's an unconscious reaction to the handling of their genitals. The easiest way to deal with it is to distract the patient, paying no attention to the obvious excitement in his groin. Perhaps it is a carry-over from childhood days of playing doctors and nurses. Either way, it's to be ignored.

When examining women, I always asked a nurse or my secretary to come into the room. I had never thought to do that when examining gay males. So many surgeons have been accused by patients of improper behaviour when their only crime is to examine the patient's pelvis or rectum. At what point does a patient start to feel uncomfortable with a private examination and infer that the doctor is making sexual overtones?

Cases of surgeons who had abused the trust placed in them always hit the papers and ended the surgeon's career.

I had always been able to stay away from these accusations and I certainly didn't want that to change today. I diverted attention elsewhere and commenced examination of his breasts. They were more prominent than I'd expected.

'Are you on any hormones?' I asked. It was common practice for transvestites to place themselves on oestrogen, a female hormone, in order to grow breasts. Gynecomastia was the medical term for growing breasts.

'I used to take a lot when I was sixteen. I gave up about a year ago because someone said it was dangerous.' This young man had spent a lifetime moulding himself into a woman. He lived as a woman, he had a woman's thoughts. Except, he was born a male. Each day as he showered or toileted, there was a constant reminder of his manhood.

'I am saving up for the operation, Doctor.' He looked so sad. He was desperate to become a woman.

'Which operation, Jo?' I feigned ignorance.

'You know, to make me a woman. They'll cut off my balls and dick and make me a vagina. That way, I'll become a woman. That's what I am. I'm a woman. It's just an accident of birth that I had to have these things down there!'

'Well, get dressed, Jo, and we can talk about the blood in your urine. That is the most important and urgent thing now.'

Avoidance of emotionally laden material – a common practice when one did not want the patient to go down a pathway that opened a Pandora's box.

Jo got dressed as I wrote up his notes.

I explained the findings on the CT scan and described the operation in detail. His major concern was whether the scar would be large afterwards. I reassured him that while it would be large and prominent at first, it would gradually become less visible. Arrangements were made. This was a curable cancer. We could certainly heal with steel. This was the catch-cry of surgeons.

The day arrived. I stood in the anaesthetic anteroom waiting for the theatre to be ready. Jo had been stripped of all adornment and was in a white gown tied at the back. He was a young boy now, not a glamorous woman. Tissues had been used to wipe many a tear. His father had bashed him numerous times during his short life. He had been gay-bashed by hooligans in his neighbourhood regularly. He had been ostracised by society as an oddity. He had to have a lot of strength to cope with all of this. Yet, here he was, helpless.

I reached out and placed my hand on his shoulder. 'I will do my best for you, Jo.'

He took my hand and held it – he was desperate for human contact. The nurse came in, looked at me oddly and announced that they were ready.

'I'll see you in there, Jo,' I called out as he was wheeled away.

I went to scrub. By the time I had finished my registrar had the patient prepped. Gowns were draped so that all we could see was a small rectangular window. Draping was done primarily to prevent unclean instruments from getting contaminated and to indicate the sterile area clearly. Perhaps it was also intended to depersonalise the patient underneath. As a surgeon, I really did not want the added pressure of knowing that the dissection I was about to do was actually on a human being. There were so many risks: clearing the large veins around which one false move meant torrential blood loss, the chances of not being able to remove the cancer, post-operative complications. If the surgeon thought of this as a person, it would be difficult to conduct these surgical procedures. One has to dissociate. Think of the technical challenge. The beauty of the anatomy. The heroic risks appreciated only by those whose hands are next to yours inside the large, gaping wound of someone's body.

The registrar looked at me expectantly. Jo was not a private patient and hence the registrar would do his operation for training purposes. I would assist him. Public patients get free healthcare. Payback: the trainee does the operation.

'OK. Come stand over here.' There is convention in surgery. The surgeon stands on the right side of the patient and the assistant on the left. That is for all surgery except deep pelvis surgery, where the surgeon reverses his position and stands on the left to gain access, assuming, of course, the surgeon is right-handed.

He picked up the scalpel. The incision was an oblique one from the middle of the side of the chest to the tip of the tenth rib. Careful dissection was then used to deepen the incision and clear tissue from around the bone. Retractors spread the wound and revealed the fat around the kidney and the cancer.

We meticulously cleared the fat and tissue from around the major vein, freeing the kidney and its attached cancer from the back of the body, the front of the abdomen, the vein, the bowels. Then the renal artery, the renal vein and the ureter must be tied. Next came the difficult and tedious task of clearing the upper pole of the kidney. This was buried in and adherent to the underside of the liver. One false move and the bleeding could be impossible to stop.

The registrar was doing well. After a couple of hours he

had exposed the adrenal vein, the last part of the upper pole to be ligated and divided. He was pulling the whole kidney firmly to get a good view to allow him to tie off the vein.

'Just take it easy. Don't pull too hard. You'll tear the vein off the vena cava,' I cautioned him.

He tied and divided the adrenal vein nicely. The kidney was now loose, but experience leads you to very carefully free it up from the last vestiges of tissue that linked it to its previous home. However, in his enthusiasm the registrar pulled out the entire kidney, forgetting about the lumbar veins – the veins that come out of the back of the body wall. Once they are torn it can be almost impossible to stop the bleeding.

'Fuck. Take the kidney out of the way!' I immediately took over.

'But it's stuck!' He was panicking.

I took over and placed my hand around the kidney. There was still a large tethering band. Another renal artery. This is a rare variation of normal and is almost impossible to spot prior to surgery. It should have been seen when the lower pole of the kidney had been cleared. Inexperience.

'Clamp, please!' I held out my hand. My scrub nurse had read my mind even before I had formulated my thoughts. She already had the clamp in my hand. A good scrub nurse is worth their weight in gold.

I passed it underneath the kidney and blindly clamped the artery. This was called operating by braille, not for the faint-hearted.

'Scissors!' They were already in my hand.

I cut the band of tissue and removed the kidney.

'Bucket!' The kidney, the cancer, the ureter, the fat, the artery and the vein were in the bucket.

'Stitch!' The scrub nurse was already attaching the stitch to the clamp and passed it to me. I looked at her and smiled. She smiled back. She knew that the registrar would be full of awe for the control and cool-headed recovery of a difficult situation. There was a reason I was the Professor and he was the trainee.

I coolly placed a figure-of-eight stitch around the lumbar vein and immediately the bleeding stopped. All was under control now. I looked at the registrar. He was shaky. He realised that had he been by himself, this patient would have died.

'Are you happy to close up?' I did not wait for the answer. 'Don't forget the drains.' I left to go to the tea room.

Jo would make an uneventful recovery. Three weeks later he was sitting in front of me in the rooms. He was in a floral linen top, a white silk skirt and high heels. Very Audrey Hepburn!

'Well, I have some good news for you. We have the pathology report. The tumour we took out is all gone and it is a benign tumour. That means it does not spread. So essentially you are cured.'

'That's great, Doctor.' Jo was still taking it all in, but was pleased.

'It is an interesting tumour. It is called an angiomyolipoma.' I was excited. He did not share my excitement.

'God. I couldn't even say it, let alone spell it,' he tittered.

'The interesting thing about these tumours, Jo, is that they are much more common in women than men.'

In front of me, Jo Tavali underwent a visible change, the like of which I rarely saw in my years of practice. His face brightened and a huge happy smile shone across his beautiful young face.

For the first time, he had validation of who he was. A large load of guilt, of rejection, of self-doubt and humiliation clearly lifted from his back.

It was the first time in his life that Jo had objective proof that he was born to be a woman.

CHAPTER 22

Father Santino

But that the dread of something after death,
The undiscover'd country from whose bourne
No traveller returns, puzzles the will
And makes us rather bear those ills we have
Than fly to others that we know not of?

FROM *HAMLET*, ACT III, SCENE I, BY WILLIAM SHAKESPEARE

Perhaps more than most other surgeons, I found myself dwelling on existentialist questions. It may have been my own religious upbringing, or my enjoyment of poetry, art and literature. Perhaps I was just odd. After my mother's death, I found myself asking questions about the patient's life, their pain, their hopes and aspirations more frequently. I would often ask what they thought awaited them in the afterlife. Did they believe in God? What was God for them?

Father Santino's case offered me more insight than most into religion. I was in my forties and was contemplating middle age. That year I bought a sports car, which I sold shortly after I had seen a reflection of myself in a shop window while waiting for a traffic light to turn green. Instead of the handsome young man that filled my fantasies, I saw a middle-aged, balding, greying man with deep wrinkles on his face, driving a car that should belong to someone 20 years younger.

The other thing that happens to a man in his forties is that thoughts of his own mortality start to creep into his psyche. You are on the downward slope to death; it seems even more inevitable. I had an aversion to religion, but not to spirituality. Believing in God, an afterlife, a spiritual dimension to life, was one thing. Being religious was another.

I had been brought up a believing yet moderate Muslim. As I grew older, my spirituality increased but my religiousness decreased. I sensed the presence of a greater being but I could not simply and blindly accept that there was only one way to heaven. Born-again Christians would proclaim to me in the street that the path to heaven was only through the blood of Jesus Christ. I thought of the Masai tribesmen whose spirituality was legendary. Were they all going to go to hell? On whose say-so? What of the awful atrocities that the people of Bosnia, of Northern Ireland, of Somalia and of the Middle East had experienced, which had been perpetrated in my lifetime in the name of religion?

What was God's position on this? Did He have a favourite religion and all others were damned? It just did not make sense. I preferred, as I grew older, to believe in God rather than in religion. Paradoxically, Islam is more tolerant of other religions than most. As George Bernard Shaw said, 'Islam is the best of religions and Muslims are the worst of followers.' World events seem to have proved him right.

Father Santino was a deeply religious man of Christian faith. He had a kindly face that made you feel he had seen God himself and that this world was nought. Death, poverty and sickness were allies that kept him in business – the religion business. He ministered to his flock and knew that he and his allies played a good-cop/bad-cop routine, preordained since ancient man had first gone to the wisest man in the village for advice. His power derived from the question humans had first asked on the plains of Ethiopia and then throughout their migration to Asia, the Nile Delta and into Europe.

Is there something after death?

Father Santino spoke to all he ministered about Heaven and Hell and the passage to the other, greener pastures. He spoke of the glorious gardens, God's grace and the life eternal.

Death was nothing more than a passage, a journey to a greater and more wonderful place. Father Santino gave the mother whose child was dying hope that the child would live on beyond the grave. He gave the man who had been swindled of his entire wealth the courage to know, beyond doubt, that justice would be his in the hereafter.

He convinced the wealthy to give charity so that they might build their life eternal as well as their life on earth. All this he did with total conviction and a face whose smile exuded warmth and serenity.

Who knew what his own personal beliefs were. Did he truly believe all he said about God and the afterlife? Did he have doubts about his own passage from this life to the next? Whatever the case, for Father Santino the truth would soon be apparent. Soon, he would be dead.

Father Santino sat across the desk from me. Next to him was a handsome young blond boy, perhaps seventeen. His name was Michael and he had come with the Father to all his appointments. He wore the sign of the fish on his lapel but the relationship between them was more intimate than I would have expected from a trainee priest and an elder.

This old, obese priest and this gorgeous young boy were perhaps lovers. I found myself wondering what rationalisation he had uttered to persuade this young man into believing that he was serving God through giving his body unto the priest. But I knew really all that mattered was that they both found happiness in their relationship, whether it be as lovers or as friends. And Father Santino was going to need all the support he could muster after I broke the news contained within the pathology results I held in my hand. Both sat there expectantly – waiting.

'I'm sorry, Father, but I do not have good news for you.' I paused, anticipating the effect of my words. They looked at each other, just as a husband and wife would do.

'There is cancer in each of the biopsies from your prostate. Also, they are a high grade. It is an aggressive cancer,' I went on.

There are times when you cannot couch it any better. I am tempted sometimes to just say, 'You are fucked.' Before me unfurled the entirety of this man's future. The metastases or spread of his cancer would first migrate to his bones and then to the rest of his body. And then came the painful death.

I can't help you any more.

Tears welled up in the young boy's eyes. Father Santino too was crying. Anguish spread across his face. He was sobbing like a child.

'Why me, Doctor? Why me? I have served God all my life. I have not questioned, I have tried to live a good life. Why me?'

I said nothing. I had heard reactions like this so many times before, but not from a priest. He was the fourth patient that day to whom I had given a death sentence, and I was exhausted. Each person has their own belief system that assists them to cope or, in some cases, detracts from their ability to cope with impending death. I wondered why a priest would not almost welcome death and the meeting with his Maker.

Michael put his arm around the priest, cuddled his head and tried to alleviate the pain in a childlike attempt to kiss it better. I suppose he was indeed little more than a child, but now he was called upon to act as a parent, as a confidant and as a companion.

People normally take time to assimilate this type of information and all the implications. This man must have known it before coming to my office. Perhaps his intense reaction was to do with Michael. No sooner had this love come into his life than the robber of his happiness – the cancer now growing in his loins – had also made its unwelcome visit.

Now he had a lover and a cancer that was incurable and would result in a life struck down.

'How long do I have, Doctor?'

'Well, it is very advanced, Father, but no one can tell with any certainty. It could be weeks. It could be months. I have seen people survive years.' I was trying to let them cling on to hope.

'Is there anything that could be done?' Michael asked, his beautiful eyes sharing the pain of Father Santino. I looked at him silently. He understood.

I was aware that I had a waiting room full of patients. I needed to give the Father time to digest this poisonous draft. He sat there, still sobbing.

'What scares you about death, Father?' I asked.

He looked at me, trying to gather together his priestly self. 'I am not afraid of death. I have lived a good life and God promises us eternal salvation.'

Then why cry? Why be afraid of death? Or was it that Father Santino did not believe what he was saying? He looked across at Michael.

Belief: that essential ingredient. You jump into your father's arms as a young child because you have an unshake-able belief that he will catch you. You traverse the divide to the afterlife with peace because you have a belief that there is something better, that there is some continuity. It matters not whether the belief is an absolute one about the existence of God, or whether the belief is atheistic. As long as there is belief. Unshakeable belief. Atheists believe that it all ends. There is nothing after death. I have always found they cope with death better than religious individuals who complicate it all with judgements to be made upon death, choices between heaven and hell, angels, prophets, God's judgement.

Will He like me? Have I done something that He finds it necessary to punish me for? Am I going to have my flesh burnt from my body for eternity? Awful images that fill the mind of the dying religious person with dread.

Guilt is the constant companion of all religious folk. The guilt of masturbation, of the indiscretion of their youth, of their transgressions over the years. As surgeons we saw the seven deadly sins played out with all their immense implications each day. We had the privileged position that otherwise only Catholic priests hearing confession have – the insights into human frailty that make what we bear more bearable. We got over guilt. This man did not seem to have this insight despite his vast religious experience.

'I have saved a bit of money, Doctor,' said Michael. 'Do you think it safe for Joe to travel? I want to take him to Lourdes. He has always wanted to go and perhaps we could see a miracle there. Our prayers are sometimes stronger than your medicines.'

Michael was a believer. I could not understand the Anglicans before me believing in Lourdes. But what the hell? I had Muslim patients with Buddhist prayer beads next to their beds; atheists whose final words are prayers to God: no greater evidence for separation of religion and belief.

'I think Lourdes would do him good. God still works miracles.' I sounded almost priestly myself. A trip to Lourdes might give them both comfort and that was all that mattered. No one said that being honest was part of the job description for a surgeon.

Father Santino stood up to go. He reached out his hand and thanked me. Then he made the sign of the cross to bless me. Images of exorcism came to mind. I wondered if my Muslim flesh would burn with the blessing. Nothing happened. In fact, it was strangely comforting. I was not the devil after all.

A few months later, Father Santino and Michael were standing before the Virgin Mary at Lourdes. Michael had emailed me about their progress. I replied to say that I would be in Paris for a conference and suggested we could meet if they were there at the same time. They were. I was so curious to see this relationship and the way that this man was handling death that I made plans to go to my conference early. I wanted to see the resolution to the questions that dogged me about Father Santino's beliefs. I still could not understand his tears at the news of his death. Here was a man going through the ordeal of his life, whose dichotomy between religion and belief was to haunt rather than comfort his final days. How would he resolve to see the face of God?

Three days before my conference, I got a message from Michael that Father Santino had been admitted to hospital in Paris and it was not looking good.

I skipped the opening ceremony of the conference and went to visit him in hospital. He was at the Hotel Dieu. I walked into the vast courtyard. In front of me was the Tomb of the Unknown Soldier honouring the hundreds of doctors, nurses and orderlies who had died in the many wars Paris had seen. Young medical students rushed by with huge texts under their arms. Visitors streamed past. I was a visitor – not a role I undertook often. I saw the statue of Charcot, the famous neurologist who had added so much to medical knowledge.

I was awed by the fact that so many famous surgeons and physicians had worked in this hospital. Etched on this city's history were some of the most fundamental discoveries in medicine, and this hospital, the Hotel Dieu, was at the heart of this history.

I found the front hall and the information desk. '*Bonjour. Je cherche a patient.*' My French was atrocious.

'*Comment il s'appelle?*' The attendant was impatient and probably spoke perfect English, but refused to.

'*Père* Joseph Santino?'

'*Ah, oui. Deuxième étage, chambre trois.*' He was already looking toward the next enquirer as he spoke. I was dismissed.

I walked to the lifts, the type with metal grates across the front that you lock in place to get the lift started. I pressed two. I could already smell the disinfectant, the faeces, the urine. I felt at home.

Room 3 was to the right. I knocked and entered. Michael was sitting on a chair next to Father Santino. I was unprepared for the sight of this frail, gaunt man. He had lost so much weight. Michael was looking very worn for a 17-year-old boy. I grabbed a chair on the other side of the bed and sat down.

'Doctor Khadra is here to see you, Father.' The eyes opened and the Father turned his head slightly. A faint smile touched his face. His lips were parched. He was spent. His Bible was on the bedside table.

'How was Lourdes?' I was trying to find conversation.

Michael eagerly told me the story. They had prayed to the Virgin Mary. They had drunk from the waters. They had gone to find a cure. On the second day of prayer, a beam of light came down from the heaven and the beam lit Father Santino's forehead. He looked up, started smiling and said, 'I am ready, my son.'

Michael had goose bumps as he told me the story. God had spoken personally to Father Santino to give him courage to face death.

I looked at the Father. He was motionless. I looked to see if there were respiratory excursions across the chest.

There were none. Michael had not yet realised what had happened. I gently moved my hand to the Father's neck.

'Is he all right, Doctor?'

I said nothing. I counted the beats. They were faint but still there. His heart was beating its last.

Shortly after this Father Santino was dead. Michael had started crying and was saying the Lord's Prayer. I joined him with the Fatihah, the first verse of the Koran. The nurse heard the sobs and came in, and a priest was called. Later, after the undertaker had visited, I asked Michael what he was going to do.

'I am going to be a priest, of course,' he said, total conviction in his face. I gave him a hug and bade him farewell.

I came out of the hospital at dawn. I had stayed with the Father and Michael all night. Father Santino wanted to be buried in France and the church would attend to all details.

In front of the hospital was the Notre Dame Cathedral. The tourists had not lined up yet and the square was empty. I waited till opening time then I went in and sat before the statue of the Virgin Mary and her child. I sat for hours as the light slowly brightened through the vast blue stained-glass window. I got up and lit a candle for Father Santino, hoping God would be kind.

I looked over to see the nuns who now were tending the altar of the blessed Mary. Had Father Santino found peace in his afterlife? Was there an afterlife?

However, I had a conference to attend. That, and the mandatory shopping trip to La Samaritaine, the big department store in Paris, was now more pressing than the afterlife.

The following week I returned home, and the existential questions came flooding back in a most affronting way.

CHAPTER 23

Ulysses

Tho' much is taken, much abides; and tho'
We are not now that strength which in the old days
Moved earth and heaven; that which we are, we are;
One equal-temper of heroic hearts,
Made weak by time and fate, but strong in will
To strive, to seek, to find, and not to yield.

'ULYSSES' BY SIR ALFRED, LORD TENNYSON

It was not a large lump, the one in the front of my neck, but a lump it was. Hard, ominous and painless. Straight out of *Bailey's Practice of Surgery*. The differential diagnosis included thyroid cancer, lymphoma and a host of awful diseases from which one did not want to die.

I really did not need this now. It was 6.30 in the morning. I was getting dressed to go to work. My career as an academic surgeon was blossoming, I had two beautiful boys, we had bought a house, I had a BMW, my wife's career was on track and she was increasing in national standing in her field. Our combined incomes meant that after such a long period of frugality, we were finally able to afford some of life's small luxuries. Skills were being honed and confidence was still rising. Life was sweet.

I felt the lump between my finger and thumb. It was certainly there, it was not my imagination. I continued to get dressed, but I could not button the top button on my shirt. I sipped some coffee and as I swallowed each gulp I felt the lump go up and down, attached to my windpipe. This was not good.

I drove to work with an awful feeling of impending doom. I was doing an outpatient session that morning. At noon, I went round to the ultrasound department. Saul Lowinsky was on.

'Hey, Saul, have you got a moment?'

'Yeah, what's up?'

'Do you think you could just run the ultrasound over my neck. I noticed a lump today. I don't think it's serious but I'd love it checked out.' I was trying to hide the urgency I felt.

'Sure, come right in. You're lucky. I have a break till one,' he said.

'Lucky,' I thought. I hope so. I lay down in my suit on the ultrasound bed. He spread gel on my neck. Then typed my details into the machine.

'OK. Just lie back and enjoy.' This was his normal patter.

Silence. Long silence. Out of the corner of my eye I could see the screen. His face suddenly looked serious. He had visibly paled.

'What can you see, Saul?' I asked, knowing what he could see.

'Well, it's a lump. Probably benign, though . . .' Saul did not want an emotional scene in his department. Who did? His job was to find tragedy, not to deal with the emotional fallout.

'Is it solid or cystic?' I was being very clinical. It was the type of conversation I would normally have with Saul about a patient he was doing an ultrasound on for me.

'Oh . . . hard to say,' he said. I could see the screen, though, and it was definitely solid. A solitary, solid tumour in the thyroid could only be one thing: a cancer.

'Saul, could you check the rest of my neck for metastases.' I was again being clinical. I had to guide him. He needed counselling. It was not easy to diagnose cancer in a colleague, a friend.

'It looks like there are some cysts up in the upper part of the neck on the left. Hold on. Yes, some on the right as well. Yes, there are some on both sides. I am sure it's nothing, mate.' He had to stop now. He was not coping.

'It's OK, Saul. I am OK. Do you think you could print those out for me.' I was cool. I felt totally in control. It was as if I was watching a patient interaction from a distance and I was managing the case. The cancer was not in me. It was in some kind of doppelganger.

Saul printed the x-rays out for me and handed them over. I went back to outpatients. I had about 20 patients waiting. I saw them all myself. Then, at 4 pm, I called Professor Lionel Dieter. He and I had written several articles on thyroid cancer together when I was his registrar. He knew more about the disease than anyone else I knew, almost anyone else in the world. He could see me at 8 pm in his rooms.

'I'm flying out to a conference tomorrow morning. This is the last thing I need,' he said.

'I am sorry, Lionel. I can see you after you are back if you prefer.' I hoped he would not say that was his preference.

'No, no, no – it's OK. Let's do a biopsy tonight. The results will be through on Friday. The ultrasound doesn't look too good, does it?'

I lay down on his examination couch. He spread some alcohol on my neck and then plunged a wide bore needle into the mass after localising it between his thumb and forefinger. I could hardly breathe. The pressure was obstructing my windpipe and the pain from the needle was almost unbearable. Is this really what we did to patients? This was painful. This was uncomfortable. This was frightening. I had done maybe a hundred of these biopsies to patients. I really did not realise they hurt this much.

He injected parts of my thyroid into a bottle and labelled it with my name. It was strange to see my name being placed on a bottle going to the pathology department. A patient's name belongs where Professor Dieter was writing my own.

I said nothing to anyone about the lump. I was distracted at home over dinner, but then I was often distracted. It was a common characteristic among surgeons. The day replayed itself as soon as you got home. Conversations with patients were had again, decisions one had made were re-examined. Were they the right decisions? It was not uncommon for my wife to ask, 'When are you coming out of your cave so we can talk?' That inevitably jolted me back to reality.

I looked at her putting full plates in front of my sons. I said nothing.

Later that night, I told her about the lump and the consultation with Dieter. She became a wife rather than a doctor. Her immediate reaction was to comfort me. We knew little, but suspected a lot.

'I really do not want to be a patient again,' I said.

'We'll cope, just like we've always coped,' she replied. With that, sleep overtook us both. We fell asleep in each other's arms, as if cuddling could keep reality out.

Little was said about this until the results were confirmed later in the week. Friday finally arrived. I waited impatiently all morning for the phone call to come from pathology. Was it cancer? Was it a benign, non-cancerous growth?

My phone went off just as I was about to scrub for a case. I went outside the theatre complex to take the call.

'Hello. This is the senior pathologist,' she said in a calm voice. 'Lionel Dieter asked me to call you immediately with the results.'

'Yes. Thank you for getting the results through so quickly. What is the news, Doctor?'

'I am afraid it's not good news. The biopsy shows sheets of papillary cells with multiple mitotic figures. The biopsy is definitely malignant. Have you made a follow-up appointment with Professor Dieter?' She needed to make sure there was follow-up arranged.

I went back into theatre and scrubbed. No one suspected the turmoil that now invaded my thoughts. I did not know whether I was going to live or die. I did know, however, that this was in the lap of the gods, and I was now at the mercy of the health system. I had to be a patient and enter mortal combat. It was my life at stake in this round.

Professor Dieter came back from his conference a week later.

'Well, just as we thought. You'll need a total thyroidectomy and neck dissection. We'll follow that up with radioiodine treatment. I have a spot for the surgery next Wednesday. My secretary will help fill out the forms. You obviously know the operation backwards so there's no need for me to perform a full informed consent. Do you have any questions? I do not expect you would.' He rattled off his usual patter to an unusual audience.

That night, both my wife and I felt it was time to let our friends know. We called them. They came round to give me comfort. Our closest friends were oncologists and they brought round volumes of information. I suddenly felt incredibly susceptible.

The more I read, the more unwell I felt. Complications, outcomes, disasters, what-ifs . . . I could not take it. I did not want this. I did not ask for this. I wanted this to go away. It was not going to go away. I was a patient. Those textbooks now referred to me, not to someone else. Those statistics were about me and 'patients' just like me.

I asked our friends to leave and my wife saw them to the door. I went in to say goodnight to my boys. I lay down next to them and read them a story. How much longer was I to be allowed to do this before this growth in my neck was to end my life? I kissed them and left. I wanted them not to know, not to worry.

I was not going to be a crier like Santino when I faced my death. I was not going to whimper out of this life. I, like Dylan Thomas's father, intended not to go quiet into that still night, but to rage and rage against the dying of the light.

I needed Mahler. Mahler's Symphony No. 2, The Resurrection. It was the only treatment I needed now. Loud, deep and unrestrained by volume control. I put my headphones on so as not to wake the children, and tried deafening myself. Maybe then I would not hear any of the statistics, the lies.

The week moved very slowly. I continued to work. I had to make arrangements for the patients.

'How long will you be away for this time, Doctor?' The outpatients' secretary was not happy to be cancelling patients at the last minute.

'About two weeks, Lisa,' I replied. She thought I was going on a conference again. I had not told her.

My wife and I sat in the waiting room of the admissions department filling out forms that revealed almost every piece of personal detail I could imagine.

'They have not asked if I wanked as a kid,' I said, in full earshot of the admissions clerk.

'Shut up and take this seriously.' My wife was not relishing the situation.

Up on the ward, the charge sister welcomed me.

'Take your clothes off. Have a shower using this antiseptic soap and then get into this gown. They'll come for you shortly. You're first on the list.'

It is hard having a surgeon as the patient. I was used to doing ward rounds, not lying down on one of the ward beds. This sister accompanied me often when I was 'the surgeon'. Now she was directing me. It was not a role she was enjoying either. The orderly came. I got onto the gurney and kissed my wife goodbye. The cannula was placed in my hand and then the anaesthetist injected my pre-med. Two hours passed in an instant.

'I can't breathe. Please let me sit up. Please let me sit up!' I was in recovery.

I had a drain in my neck to stop post-operative bleeding obstructing my breathing passage. The tube was so uncomfortable. I had intense pain radiating from my neck. I was nauseated.

'Please give me a bowl.' The nurses were coming in and out of focus.

The next few hours were a blur. My wife holding my hand, the nurses coming in and out of my room. Pain, nausea, migraine, dizziness. I focused again around midnight. I needed to urinate so I pressed the buzzer. No one came. I pressed the buzzer again. I got up out of bed, dragged my drip stand and my drain to the toilet and sat down to urinate. I was alive. I could not remember being more ill than I felt at that moment.

Is this really what patients felt? It was a long while since I had witnessed the aftermath of our operations. As residents and registrars we saw patients on the night of surgery. Yes, I remember them being ill. However, did they feel as badly as I felt now? I suddenly felt very sorry for every single soul that I had operated on. Was this payback? There was obviously a God and I was now being punished for my sins. What was my crime? The pain in my neck was intense. The pain in my head was even worse.

I went back to bed. I suddenly realised that this was the bed where a patient I had grown very fond of had died. He had died of bladder cancer. I remembered that the cancer had fungated into his rectum and this room was filled with the smell of faeces long after he had passed. For that reason alone, it was hard to visit with him. The bed was always soaked with faeces. I did not want to get back in bed, but I was about to faint.

At 7 am there was a change of shift. No nurses can be had at change of shift. Handover was a hallowed hour in every hospital. Please do not arrest now. Please do not press the buzzer now. Please keep your heart going now. Please keep your lungs breathing now. We are in handover. One shift telling the next that you are to live or you are about to die.

The morning observations started shortly afterwards. A young male nurse came in to take my pulse and blood pressure. The idea was to make sure he documented that I was still alive.

'It was a great party last night,' he shouted to a fellow nurse across the hallway.

I looked up at him. He had tattoos on his left forearm; a skull and crossbones in his left ear dangled down. He had a mohawk haircut.

'How are you feeling?' he asked carelessly.

'I am in a lot of pain. Could I have a painkiller?' I had needed a painkiller for several hours now.

'I'll get some as soon as I finish my observations, OK?' He had already moved on to the next patient.

No, it is not OK. I need it now!

I said nothing. I waited another hour for my pain relief.

'Time for a shower. Upsy-daisy.' It was the mohawk nurse again. He helped me up to the bathroom.

'Do you need help?' he asked, hoping I would say no.

'No, I'm fine.' I turned on the water. There was a shower curtain that had been white once. The bath had yellow streaks where the tap had leaked for several years. I got under the shower and the curtain clung to my body, drawn in by the heat. I could not take it any more. How many open sores had this curtain hugged? How many wounds, infections, colostomies? How many patients had received their last hug from this curtain?

Hot tears rolled out from my eyes. I started sobbing, crying like a baby. I squatted in the bath. The water mixing with my tears was flowing down the drain hole. Small droplets of blood mixed with the tears, with the water. I could not stay upright. My head felt like it was about to blow. I needed to find comfort in this place of discomfort. I did not want to be a lump of meat in a bed. I am a surgeon, I am a man. I have a man's needs.

Here was the full ugliness of the healthcare system unleashed on me. Did God not know that I had struggled against it all my life? Did God not know that I was the one exposing its shortcomings and helping to train medical students to do it better? Here was the full effect of outsourced cleaning. I wanted to get out of that hospital. I wanted to be in my shower, my bed, my room. '*Please do not let me die here*,' was my constant prayer.

I got out of the shower and dried myself. I called my wife, who came straight in. Professor Dieter saw me shortly afterwards on his morning ward rounds.

'There was a lot of cancer in your neck. You'll need radio-iodine to mop up the rest. That means you'll be radioactive for about two weeks. No contact with family, I'm afraid.' He was matter-of-fact.

As he announced this, a hospital workman was changing the light globe above me. Small bits of ceiling fell on my bed. I flicked them off and stared at the wall in front of me.

Countless family pictures stuck to the wall with Sellotape had lifted off tiny flecks of paint. They'd been put there by patients who announced to all who cared to see that they had families, that they were loved. Poems from grandchildren, get-well cards from wives, children's drawings. It was as if there was a need in the hospital to announce one's humanity, to shout out, 'I am a human being!'

Shakespeare's *Merchant of Venice* came to mind: Shylock convincing the audience that he is human despite being a Jew. 'Hath not a Jew eyes? Hath not a Jew hands, organs, dimensions, senses, affections, passions? Fed with the same food, hurt with the same weapons, subject to the same diseases, healed by the same means, warmed and cooled by the same winter and summer as a Christian is? If you prick us, do we not bleed? If you tickle us, do we not laugh? If you poison us, do we not die?'

Lunch arrived: a concoction of spiced minced beef with a bread roll served on a disposable paper plate. As I ate the mince, painfully swallowing each mouthful, I realised that bits of the cardboard that constituted my plate were dissolving into the food. I had actually eaten a hole straight through and was eating my mince off the green plastic tray below. I pushed it away from me.

Across the hall, Mrs Perry, my renal cancer patient, was dying. She had metastases in her brain, back and lungs and was wasting away to a shadow as each cancerous cell multiplied in two, and then four and then eight, until the next doubling of cells meant the difference between life and death. Mrs Perry had reached the end of the line. Chemotherapy, radiotherapy, surgery, immunotherapy, she had had it all. Now she lay in a comatose state, the family sitting around waiting for the inevitable, having already planned the funeral and divided the assets.

I hoped against hope that the family would not recognise me and come over to see me in the state I was in. The surgeon must maintain control, imperviousness, the barrier. That was all we had between the quagmire of suffering in which we lived our lives and survived as human beings.

Six weeks later, I was in the isolation ward for my radio-iodine. No human contact for ten days. No hugs, no kisses, no sharing of utensils. It was the worst kind of sensory deprivation.

Despite the treatments, the surgery and the neck dissection, my cancer continued to grow. I could not listen any more. My wife took it all in and guided me. I would need to have more surgery and probably more radioiodine. It was far worse the second time round. By the end of nearly six months of medical and surgical treatment I was a physical disaster. It had been worth it, though. My cancer was under control, for the moment.

During my recovery, I continued to operate, to see patients and to teach. I had taken only a few days' leave, most of these only when I was hospitalised.

When I was a resident, I once had the flu. I struggled to work with a temperature over 39 degrees. I was sick. In the lift with my boss, I said, 'I came as close as I have ever come to taking a day's sick leave today.' He stepped up to me, looked right in my eyes and said, 'Son, you take a day's sick leave and you will never become a surgeon.'

Still, to this day, I look down on doctors who take time off. For me, the worst offenders are those that take stress leave, whatever that may be. I have always lived by the aphorism that 'stress is good for you, it flushes the coronary arteries'.

Cancer never leaves a person the same as they were before. It imbues a certain paranoia about mortality that is impossible to shake. The enemy is within. Every lump, every headache, every bone pain is a possible recurrence. Each day, one lives with this impending mortality, knowing that the next day could be the last.

The Sufis stress the constant cognition of mortality. Live each day knowing that all actions are recorded, all deeds count. The ultimate sword of Damocles hanging above my head, your head, everyone's heads.

Colleagues found out through the hospital grape-vine. They had the usual reaction we, as doctors, have to colleagues who are sick – an over-compensatory sorriness that was meant to allay the distaste they felt that I had now joined the 'others', the patients. I was no longer invincible like they were.

Of all the diseases, cancer seems to create super-sensitive radar in the patient for the falseness of feigned compassion. Real care and genuine concern are rare. I really preferred people to just ignore my ordeal rather than to ask a battery of sillitudes (a word I made up at the time).

My patients, on the other hand, seemed almost relieved. It was as if the fallen angel made their ordeal more bearable, and my illness made doctors appear more human; this susceptibility behind the mask was a comfort to them. *'We knew you were not perfect after all!'* Perhaps they also felt that I would have more compassion towards them, more under-standing of their ordeals.

I certainly did have more knowledge of pain, of human suffering, of doubt and of self-analysis. My ability to relate to the genuine suffering among my patients increased dramati-cally. There were times after my cancer when I could hardly stand the pain that they suffered. I knew what it felt like to have injection after injection, accumulations of discomfort that then became intolerable. I knew that the simple CT scan with intravenous contrast I ordered with impunity was actually an uncomfortable experience; that lying on a bed outside an operating theatre waiting your turn is a few of the most frightening minutes a human being can spend, like a child sitting on a potty in a sea of snakes. Helplessness in the extreme.

On the other hand, I also knew to detect those patients who used their illness as a means to sympathy. I despised them. 'There are so many who are worse off than you. Get up and get a hold of yourself.'

Most importantly, the barriers between my own inner sanctum of protection and the patient's suffering had broken down. It was impossible to be dispassionate. It was impossible not to feel the patient's illness as if it were my own. I knew then that my days in surgery were numbered. Each day I died again, was operated on again, felt the pain of stitches again, felt the utter helplessness again. It was not sustainable. I could not stand the pain of the cognisance of life's finiteness. Everything reminded me of my mortality. Perhaps that's why the timing of a person's death is such a mystery. Perhaps that's why we all live in denial. It is the only bearable way for life to continue.

In the months that followed my illness, I found myself drawn to the idea of leaving surgery. At first I suppressed my musings. I also sought the company of other doctors who had shared my fate, who themselves had experienced illness. One such doctor was Bernard Schulz, an old surgeon who was nicknamed the 'Captain' because he barked orders constantly.

CHAPTER 24

O Captain! My Captain!

O Captain! my Captain! our fearful trip is done,
The ship has weathered every rack, the prize we sought is won,
The port is near, the bells I hear, the people all exulting,
While follow eyes the steady keel, the vessel grim and daring;
But O heart! heart! heart!
O the bleeding drops of red,
Where on the deck my Captain lies,
Fallen cold and dead!

FROM 'O CAPTAIN! MY CAPTAIN!' BY WALT WHITMAN

Dr Bernard Schulz walked the corridors of the hospital, striding, as does the captain on the bridge of a warship. However, today his walk was that of the defeated Napoleonic soldiers returning, barely alive, from the Russian front. You can tell a lot about doctors from the way they walk. The careful tread of the neurologist, measuring every nuance of each step. The sports-injured knee of the orthopaedic surgeon with arms held out wide from the body and palms facing backwards. The languid amble of the palliative-care physician for whom there is never a need to rush.

Today, Bernard Schulz was not in command. This was his last day in the Victoria Hospital. He was a man with a timebomb ticking away inside him. His oncologist had advised that his lymphoma – diagnosed and treated four years previously – had recurred and that the only possible course of action was high-dose, toxic chemotherapy. The oncologist had shown him the statistics. He told him that there was a 20 per cent chance of remission and no chance of a cure. He was being optimistic. Bernard Schulz knew that his time was up. He knew death was nigh.

The price for the treatment as suggested would be three months of nausea, vomiting, sickness and toxaemia. Arrangements had been made for Dr Schulz to start chemotherapy the following week. But Dr Schulz had other plans. He was simply not going to undergo the treatment. He had already planned his death. He was going home.

He had walked these corridors for over 40 years. He had started at the Victoria Hospital as a medical student; he had trained as a surgeon here and was then an assistant Honorary before becoming a staff member. As a surgeon, he had put his name to several new operations in the seventies that had attracted international recognition. He had patients on his books going back over his whole career.

It was easier in the old days. The technology was simpler. There were no computers. Administrators worked for the hospital and on behalf of the staff and patients, rather than working on their careers. Keyhole surgery was unknown.

Surgeons did not charge public patients or the elderly. A private patient was the sustenance by which you financially survived. The public hospital was the place you gave service to humanity and to the community.

Then came the Medicare reforms of the late seventies and early eighties. Doctors had to keep timesheets in order to be paid. Dr Schulz regarded pharmaceutical and medical insurance companies as the greatest of all evils in society. They pushed their products and incited patients to sue doctors and to expect care that was not humanly possible to give.

His patient notes were held in metal files, each in its own separate A5 envelope. When computers came to medicine, he resisted all attempts to modernise his practice. His secretaries still typed his letters on old Olympus electric typewriters. He refused to provide word processors. His accounts were conducted on a ledger of transactions. He bought a new one each year and the dollars and cents always tallied perfectly.

He looked at young specialists starting out with great amusement. They borrowed money to establish their practice. He had borrowed the dining-room chairs from home and used them in his waiting room. His desk was purchased from the government stores and was still sturdy.

His patients had been loyal and surgery had been good to him. He had educated his four children in private schools and had a small place by the beach. His house was paid off.

I saw him walking in the distance down the corridor and guessed what was going through his mind. I thought twice about it and then greeted him as I neared. 'Good morning, Doctor Schulz.' Even though I had trained under this man, and was a colleague, I had never been able to call him Bernard. He inspired too much respect. He looked up as if I had woken him from a deep sleep.

'Morning.' He was more tired and haggard than I had ever seen him before.

'Are you OK?'

'Yes, thank you.' He was often abrupt. He was from the old school where the surgeon's motto was 'No excuses, no apologies!'

'Are you going to be able to come to the seminar next week? I would really value your comments on some of the registrar presentations,' I asked. I was always trying to involve him in the hospital's activities.

The registrar research seminar was a yearly event, and being one of the organisers meant that I had the task of finding a panel to judge their efforts. From the registrars' point of view, it was viewed with a polarity that depended on whether they relished the research they had been doing, which was an integral part of their training, or whether they regarded it as an imposition that was nothing more than a graft on an otherwise busy schedule.

The result was a tapestry of rehashed ideas into which the occasional golden thread of originality shone bright. The registrar who presented the best research was awarded the coveted research prize. I had won it as a registrar and it was an honour to now be organising the event.

I wanted one of my mentors, my father figure, to be there to see it.

'I am not sure I'll be able to. Today is my last day here . . .' A melancholy look passed over this tough man's face.

'I didn't know that, I thought you weren't retiring until late next year?' I knew the story, but feigned ignorance. 'Do you have time for a cup of coffee?' I did not have time, but I felt that this man needed to talk.

He looked down at his watch out of habit. I knew he had time. He no longer had an operating list. That had been taken from him a couple of years ago when someone in administration felt they needed to rationalise the lists without regard to status, length of service or any other factors. Schulz's theatre time was stripped from him and given to orthopaedics. There was a greater need for that resource over there instead of here. A great wave of rationalisation swept away everything in its path without compassion or regard, with the exception of what could be recorded on paper. Dedication, loyalty, compassion, excellence, patient care; they were only relevant if they could be added or subtracted on a ledger.

This flood of rationalisation in the healthcare system was accompanied by a cancer-like growth of administration that crippled the health budget. At the Victoria Hospital there was a 30 per cent reduction in the number of beds and, at the same time, a 300 per cent growth in the number of administrative personnel. In Schulz's time there were no more than half a dozen administrators at most, and each could make decisions. The state-government bureaucracy had converted this to a mass of over a thousand administrators, none of whom could make a decision. Instead of problems being managed and resources being rationed fairly, the catchcry was 'feasibility study'. This was the mechanism by which the weak, spineless administrators who could not spell leadership, let alone practise it, came to a decision.

When a surgeon required a new piece of equipment, he used to tell the medical superintendent of the need and this would be budgeted into the next round of funding. In any hospital today, the same action would require a business plan to be written. This business plan would be considered at a number of procurement meetings attended by those whose job it was to attend meetings as a means of avoiding work. If the business plan was regarded as adequate, then a feasibility study might be conducted. Medical engineering would need to evaluate the numerous alternatives on the market and decide on the consistency and safety of this particular piece of equipment.

Then a consultant would be employed to conduct the feasibility study on the recommendation from medical engineering. Finally, the purchase would be scheduled for the next bout of funding. The whole process might cost between four and five times the actual cost of the much-needed piece of equipment. The only place where economic rationalism did not apply was to the administrators.

If you are a good clinical nurse then you get promoted to administration. The worst-paid job is to look after patients. This means shift work, low pay, and the hardship of seeing patients suffer first-hand. However, as an administrator, you wear a suit, you work nine-to-five, and patients became depersonalised numbers on a page. Far less noxious. No wonder it was the fastest growing industry in the hospital. Scaling the heights to become a State Health Department administrator was the ultimate plateau, where even the smell of antiseptic faded.

Schulz was a victim of this whole economic rationalism. He did not know, nor did he wish to know, how to write a business case for his job to be preserved. We walked past the portraits of various Professors of Surgery long gone.

'Your picture will be up there one day,' he said. He always had high hopes for me.

He was looking at me sadly. 'I gave forty years to this hospital and there has not been one word of thanks. Not one of those bastards up in Mahogany Row has come down to say thank you for your service, have a good retirement . . . nothing. No cake, no speeches, no valedictory function of any kind . . . this is not the health system I used to know.'

I agreed with him and he knew I shared his thoughts and his dismay. 'I know, Doctor Schulz. It lacks a compassion, shows a disregard for life that is destructive.'

We walked past the old wooden column that stood in the entrance of the building that had been the resident medical officer accommodation for over 100 years, until administration had taken it over to accommodate its burgeoning numbers.

'When I was an intern we had to live here, you know. If we had a day off, we would still have to be back by midnight to do a heparin round. We did everything in those days. We had to do our own pathology – our own blood smears. We spun the urine and looked down the microscope to diagnose the pathogens before starting patients on antibiotics.' He had stopped now and was caressing the column which stood at the bottom of the stairs leading up to the bedrooms that were now offices.

'George Smith and I snuck girls in through that back door once,' he said, breaking into a rare smile. 'We nearly lost our jobs over it. God, we had good times. It made it all bearable. There's no fun in it now. It's just run by them,' he nodded his head towards the top of the stairs as he spoke.

I was silent, deeply engrossed. His right hand was moving around the sides of the column. Here was a living reminder of the tragedies of economic rationalism. This column had stood for over a hundred years. Surrounding it was a tradition that was deeply ingrained in this hospital's history. Each year, when registrars and residents sat for their final examinations in the college of their speciality, the names of the successful ones were written on a piece of paper by Jim, the bar attendant, and the piece of paper was tacked to the side of this column.

The wood had had a million thumb-tack marks in it. Each was the hopes, the glory and the ambitions of a doctor fulfilled. I remembered the day my name went up. Red Texta on a piece of lined paper. Beautifully written. '*Surgical Fellowship Examinations. Congratulations. Mohamed Khadra FRACS.*'

I wept with joy when I saw it, as did almost every doctor when they saw their own name. You knew that there would be that simple acknowledgement waiting for you back at the hospital when you returned from the exams. The resident quarters were where the resident bar was situated. On Friday afternoons, all the doctors of the hospital would call in on the way home to have a pint. It was a tradition that had lived as long as the hospital had.

When administration took the building over they had commissioned a carpenter to putty up the holes in the banister because it was unsightly. With it, they puttied the optimism and commitment of almost every doctor in the hospital.

We walked on to the cafeteria.

'There was a time when there was silver-service afternoon tea served here.' Dr Schulz looked around the shabby walls of the staff cafeteria. The serving lady behind the counter continued to wipe the surface in front of her with no acknowledgement that we were standing there waiting.

We were joined in the queue by one of the new generation of surgeons whose keen awareness of the business of surgery placed him ahead of the pack. He oozed charm from every pore and had a huge following of patients. It was a pity his surgical skills did not match his charm.

'Availability before affability before ability. Every time,' whispered Dr Schulz. He had read my mind. That old aphorism had stood the test of time. We smiled together.

'Good day, boys,' said the young surgeon as he grabbed a pre-packaged salad. The serving lady gave him an expectant smile. 'How are you, my lovely darling?' She lapped it up, tittering as she handed him his change. Her toothless smile turned to disdain as she looked over to us.

'Yes?'

'Two coffees please,' Dr Schulz said.

'Just help yourselves over there. Sugar is on the tables.' More economic rationalism. There was a slot-operated coffee machine now in the staff cafeteria that replaced the served variety.

*

Dr Schulz never returned to the hospital. A week later, as I listened to registrar after registrar giving, for the most part, their inane presentations, Dr Schulz died in his bed at home. He had called his family together on the weekend and farewelled them with a dinner of legendary proportions. His coveted wine cellar yielded its aged best.

He then went to bed, surrounded by Verdi's 'Requiem' reverberating in his very soul. Dr Bernard Schulz injected himself with morphine to blunt the pain and allowed his lymphoma to quietly invade his body. He died with dignity and with courage.

Requiem aeternam dona eis, Domine, et lux perpetua luceat eis.

Eternal rest, given them, Oh Lord, and light perpetual.

CHAPTER 25

Malpractice

Two loves I have, of comfort and despair,
Which like two spirits do suggest me still;
The better angel is a man right fair,
The worser spirit a woman coloured ill.
To win me soon to hell my female evil
Tempteth my better angel from my side,
And would corrupt my saint to be a devil,
Wooing his purity with her foul pride.
And whether that my angel be turned fiend,
Suspect I may, yet not directly tell;
But being both from me, both to each friend,
I guess one angel in another's hell.
Yet this shall I ne'er know, but live in doubt,
Till my bad angel fire my good one out.

'SONNET 144' BY WILLIAM SHAKESPEARE

No matter how thick-skinned a doctor is, nothing irritates, upsets and erodes one's confidence more than a letter appearing from a patient's lawyer. There are times when a doctor has been genuinely remiss. Removing the wrong breast, the one without the cancer, is a disaster and the patient seeks compensation out of anger, out of a sense of revenge, or maybe because they also need to secure their children's future now that their treatment has gone off the rails and they face death. Cases where the doctor has been totally negligent account for a minority of the matters that are dealt with in the medicolegal courts.

Regardless of the motivation of the patient seeking redress, the doctors in question have already beaten themselves into a psychological pulp. 'How could I have done that? I'm not good enough, I do not belong in surgery, my career is over!'

However, there are lawyers whose livelihoods thrive by encouraging dissatisfied patients to sue. These lawyers advertise widely, including in hospital lifts and public toilets. These ambulance chasers have sullied the noble profession of law and are regarded negatively by both their colleagues and certainly by the medical profession.

Miss Spencer was not happy with me. She was a 50-year-old widow with a mass of uncertain origin in her kidney. She was referred to me for review. All my investigations had been unsuccessful in finding the cause. This was neither because I was a bad surgeon nor because I was negligent, but because I could not find a cause despite my best efforts. Biopsies had not revealed the nature of the mass and nor had radiological investigations.

Eventually, one is left with only one course, to remove the kidney. The worry is that there is only a 3 per cent chance the mass in the kidney is benign and a 97 per cent chance it is a cancer. The operation to take out a kidney is not minor and entails removal of the entire packet of tissue surrounding the organ without breaching the fascial layer wound so there is no possibility of spread.

Miss Spencer sailed through the operation. One week later the pathology report came back. Benign. The kidney had not had to come out.

'How could you have not known this before the operation, Doctor?' Her tone was indignant and accusatory.

'We did discuss this in detail, Miss Spencer, prior to the operation. There was no way to know for certain.' My reassuring voice resonated in the room, to no avail.

'Oh. That's terrible! There's no reason to remove a kidney if it's perfectly functional,' said Solicitor Jacob Williams. 'You should get him for that. This is a cut and dry case of gross negligence. Look at the emotional state you're in. What about the potential long-term psychological scarring of only having one kidney, not to mention the physical implications? What would happen if the other kidney should fail? You'd be unable to work, care for yourself. This is unacceptable.'

'Well, you should've seen the bill. Why should I be paying for treatment I didn't even need in the first place?'

The truth is that, on average, patients retain less than 10 per cent of the advice they receive from their caregiver. There was a time when you just told patients what they needed to know and they assumed that the doctor had their best interests at heart. If you needed a procedure, the assumption was that the doctor did not recommend an unnecessary operation. Now the trend is to ensure complete informed consent.

Informed consent means that the doctor lays out the rationale for the surgery, the procedure that will be followed, and the risks of doing the surgery while making sure that a full disclosure of all likely and important risks is detailed thoroughly. The patient should also know the risk of not having the surgery. Thereafter the patient consents to the operation only after analysing the pros and cons.

The reality is that you start with an anatomy lesson, trying to make sure the words that you have spent fifteen to twenty years learning can be understood by the patient, whose educational background may be hardly more than primary-school level. Then you go into the risks and watch them pale into a worried faint. After that they usually say, 'You do what you think is right, Doctor.'

The doctor appreciates the vote of confidence except, in the back of your mind, the awareness of the statistics nags you out of being lulled into a false sense of security. Thirty per cent of patients sue doctors because they allege the doctor failed to inform them.

'I never would've had that operation if I had known I would be left with a scar . . .'; 'If I'd known it may not work . . .'; 'If I'd known I might go slightly deaf . . .'; 'If I'd known I might become impotent . . .'

Doctors now resort to long and laborious consent procedures where patients sign that they fully understand and comprehend the likely risks. The medical insurance companies have had to raise premiums to legendary status. An obstetrician might pay in excess of 30–40 per cent of their gross income in insurance. This forces them to raise their fees. This increases both the level of dissatisfaction and the likelihood of being sued.

The lie that has been perpetrated and swallowed by the general populus is that medicine is an exact science. Lawyers talk about contracts and torts as if the doctor can control the actions of the patient's body. Surgeons have very different machines to work on than car mechanics, where the variables are totally controllable and where, if a contract is made to fix the car and it is not fixed, it is likely that the mechanic has been negligent. With surgeons, everything could be done well and the outcome could be lousy. There is often no way of controlling the variables in what is, after all, the most complex machine on earth – the human body. The body is unpredictable: it is a living, organic thing. Yet lawyers attempt to convince patients that the doctor is negligent if a certain outcome is not achieved.

Modern medicine has made the process of childbirth far safer than the misadventures of yesteryear. Yet doctors must carry a huge insurance bill to protect themselves from mothers who feel that their child's birth was imperfect. While it is always a tragedy when a child is born with malformation or even hypoxic brain damage, it does not necessarily reflect on the doctor. The baby was born mentally retarded due to oxygen starvation. Who do I blame? . . . The doctor? What patients often fail to realise is that the simplest of procedures can have complications.

My standard consent patter for even the most minor of operations starts off with, 'You can die, you can have a heart attack, you can have a stroke and you can have a clot on the lung. Now to the specifics of your operation . . .' Patients often just laugh out loud. Well, they have been warned. I write it down in my notes. I record it on the recording machine. I make contemporaneous notes. Because patients sue.

Even a simple ureteric stone may be impossible to remove one day and easy to the next. If it happens that second time round a surgeon draws the long ureteric-stone straw and the body offers up the stone like an oyster willingly offering up its pearl, the patient goes around destroying the reputation of the first surgeon, who was unable to remove it.

'He could not do the job. Thank God I got a second opinion from my new surgeon. He was able to get my stone out easily. The other surgeon is a butcher.'

*

Miss Spencer was back in Jacob Williams' office a week later. He had whipped her up into a frenzy of discontent, but she was feeling pangs of guilt for the devastation that was about to be wreaked on me. 'Are you sure he's not going to be offended? He was very compassionate towards me. It's just that I felt he should've known the operation was unnecessary.'

Williams was at his finest, soothing best. 'Don't worry. Doctors are used to being sued. He will just take this in his stride.'

The truth is, I had spent an inordinate amount of time worrying about Miss Spencer. Her kidney mass was puzzling. I had never seen anything like it. For all intents and purposes, the chances were that this was cancer, and yet it had proven not to be.

The letter was spread over several pages. Williams' letterhead, adorned with very credible and well-chosen fonts, gave the header an air of gravitas. Claims for everything from the emotional distress of misdiagnosis to gross negligence in not being able to remove a stone were levied.

After months of letters, responses and investigations, the case was thrown out and I was cleared.

Regardless of how well-prepared a surgeon is for being sued, it is an emotional and devastating event. What lawyers have succeeded in doing is converting the patient into the enemy for most doctors. We now practise defensive medicine. It used to be OK for a GP to diagnose your headache as a migraine and see how it went. Rarely, the headache is a brain tumour without the usual symptoms and signs. However, society's message to the doctor is, 'you cannot and must not get it wrong, else you will get sued'. So now the patient who comes in with a headache will, more than likely, end up with a CT scan of the head. This is not done because the headache warrants further investigation but because the doctor is 'covering his arse'. This defensiveness imposes a cost on the health system that is immeasurable.

I can recall a number of cases that have been brought against doctor colleagues of mine by lawyers like Williams. There was the 89-year-old Italian lady who needed an anaesthetic. She had one solitary tooth left in her upper jaw. During the preliminary preparation she was advised that she would need intubation during the procedure and that the tube may knock the tooth out. The tooth was already very loose.

'No problem, Doctor, I have an appointment to get dentures anyway,' she said reassuringly.

The inevitable happened. The patient's single tooth was knocked out. The doctor was sued by the family for negligence and the compensation was to pay for the dentures.

Defensive medicine. Should the anaesthetist have risked the patient's life by not intubating her or should she have just accepted the inevitable. The defence attorneys always reassure the doctor, 'This is not personal, it is the law.' The law has nothing to do with who was right or wrong, it has nothing to do with justice.

It always reminds me of the scene in the *Godfather* movie when Michael Corleone condemns his father's bodyguard to death because he had betrayed the family. The bodyguard looks at Michael and says, 'It was only business, Mikey, only business.'

Defensive medicine is not safe medicine. It is erroneous to think that the more investigations a patient undergoes, the better the treatment. Often it is the reverse. However, if I feel an abdomen and do not feel a mass, how do I know there is or isn't a mass? Do a CT scan. But what are the chances there is a mass that I have missed versus the chances that the patient will die of anaphylactic shock from the contrast iodine agent that is used during the CT scan?

Take Tom, a 40-year-old patient who walked into casualty because he had pruritus ani (an itchy arse). He had spent several hours patiently waiting in the room of the emergency department and was eventually seen at midnight.

The surgical resident who saw him analysed his condition. It was probably haemorrhoids and some cream would be all that was required, with a follow-up appointment. However, the resident was concerned about the rare chance that this could be an anal cancer with external itching as the only sign, so he decided to investigate this by performing a sigmoidoscopy. This is a minor procedure where a metal tube is inserted into the rectum through the anus in order to inspect the mucosa of the rectum and ensure that there are no lesions.

He positioned Tom on his side, explained to him what he was about to do and then commenced the procedure. He thought he could see something just beyond the limit of his scope in the upper rectum and so the resident pushed the scope a bit further up. Unfortunately, he pushed it clean out of the bowel.

Now the patient had an itchy arse and a hole in his bowel. This needed a laparotomy to open up the abdomen and repair the hole in the bowel. When they opened him up that night, they found that there was gross contamination of the peritoneum with faeces from the hole that had been inadvertently caused by the previous sigmoidoscopy. His abdomen was washed out and he was placed on high-dose antibiotics.

Over the next day or so, his sepsis became severe despite the antibiotics. Specialists were called in to review the poor man. His antibiotics were changed to no avail. The sepsis became so overwhelming that his lungs developed fluid and he was unable to breathe on his own.

He was transferred to ICU, where a tube was inserted into his throat to help him breathe. This was later made into a formal tracheostomy to allow him to live on a ventilator. The sepsis invaded his heart valves and small emboli of bacteria and clot shot off from his heart valves to various parts of his body. He had a brain abscess; he lost part of his kidneys and parts of his toes and fingers.

Seven months later, after an ordeal of pain and devastation, he left hospital, barely able to speak because of his strokes, missing several toes and fingers and needing kidney dialysis.

As he sat in his own bed for the first time in seven months, he unconsciously reached down under his pyjamas and scratched his arse.

CHAPTER 26

Passing the Torch

How dare one say it?
After the cycles, poems, singers, plays,
Vaunted Ionia's, India's – Homer, Shakespeare – the long, long times,
*   thick dotted roads, areas,*
The shining clusters and the Milky Ways of stars – Nature's pulses
*   reaped,*
All retrospective passions, heroes, war, love, adoration,
All ages' plummets dropped to their utmost depths,
All human lives, throats, wishes, brains – all experiences' utterance;
After the countless songs, or long or short, all tongues, all lands,
Still something not yet told in poesy's voice or print – something
*   lacking,*
(Who knows? the best yet unexpressed and lacking.)

'THE UNEXPRESSED' BY WALT WHITMAN

The final-year medical students slowly filtered into the auditorium, teetering on the precipice of their lives as doctors. The Professorial Tutorials in Surgery were a tradition that stretched back to Hippocrates. By final year, the student had learned anatomy, physiology, biochemistry, pathology and histology. They then marched through most of the basic specialties – gynaecology, paediatrics, basic surgery and medicine.

Theoretically, they would now command a thorough knowledge of the basics of medicine. They knew the mechanics of examining a patient and knew how to observe, palpate, auscultate and percuss their way through the body's systems. They knew the contents of their texts, each tome a life's work for which they had been allotted a defined and short time in which to imbibe the wisdom of the ages therein contained.

Some of them were still incompetent while others had retained the knowledge that would allow them to pass into medical practice. My tutorials were meant to assist them in bringing together the vast theory held in their brain cells into practical applications that would allow them to function as safe and responsible interns.

Some were dressed in designer clothing, the product of rich parents and rich private schools. Some, as was the fashion, dressed shabbily. Others arrived late with the disdain and lethargy of students who have for too long been regarded as special by families proud of their chosen careers and their achievements. Little did they realise that they were minnows, the low fragments of a long and distinguished pecking order. As interns, next year they would be even lower on the pecking order than they were now.

None of them knew that this was my last tutorial. I had finally made the decision to leave medicine and surgery behind. It was not a sudden epiphany. I had gradually made my mind up to give up surgery after my illness; after a slow build-up of pain and anguish that was impossible to live with any longer. Litigation, illness, death, failed expectations – they all took their toll. My decision to leave had crept up like a shaft of light in an otherwise dark and sad existence, like the soprano voice in Faure's requiem singing 'Pie Jesu'. Only my wife knew of my intentions.

Surgery had defined my essence as a human being and at first I could not even envisage my feelings at turning my back on it. But each night thoughts of leaving, of deserting my post, came into my mind. After a while I stopped suppressing them. I started imagining a life without surgery. I could see an existence that did not include me describing myself as a surgeon. It was a faint, ghostly image, but an image nonetheless.

Each time I operated, I was no longer detached. Empathy is the ability to acknowledge another's suffering without feeling it yourself. Over the previous years since my cancer, my ability to show empathy had gradually ceased. I was now sympathetic to every patient's suffering and anguish – sympathetic to their pain. But I felt it myself. As I put stitches in the skin to end an operation, I could visualise, almost physically feel, the pain the patient would have upon waking from the anaesthetic that now dulled their senses. I felt the debilitation of nausea, the sadness of hearing the news, the sudden realisation that one's children were soon to be orphaned. I was no longer able to practise my craft with the quiet detachment of Androcles, pulling the thorn out of the lion's paw. Each day was filled with a thousand cuts and a hundred sorrows. Each day took a new toll on my psyche and made me less effective as a surgeon.

I would stare for hours at portraits of past surgeons along the dusty corridors of the Victoria Hospital and imagine their last day. They all must have had a last day. What did it feel like to know that you could no longer push arrogantly past the plastic swinging doors that marked the opening to the theatre complex, that you were once again a member of the public outside the surgical inner sanctum? How did you live without surgery in your life?

I cast thoughts to other interests that defined who I was and education immediately sprang to mind. I felt uncomfortable with the various models of education that are exported from the developed countries to the developing countries, where being able to afford to learn is a luxury rather than a right. I decided to create my own higher-education provider, to deliver higher education to those around the world who were unable to afford it.

In each of the developing countries, the rich send their best and brightest to the West for education. In those countries, the poor have no options when it comes to getting education. They need a system that caters to them, which creates opportunities for them to change their lives and to achieve their dreams. I knew a lot about distance education and thought I could make a difference.

I made my decision. I toyed only briefly with assisting or some part-time involvement in surgery. Fundamentally, the training won . . . 'When in doubt, cut it out'. So I did. I decided to quit.

However, the students before me were not to know. Today, I was still a surgeon. I was still their infallible Professor of Surgery. I commenced my tutorial. 'OK. Who has prepared a case?' I commanded the scene. A tall blond Scandinavian put up his hand.

There was silence now. Notebooks were out. Pens standing ready in case I uttered some wisdom that would help them in their examinations.

'Yes. Uh-huh.' He was nervous. I had a reputation for not putting up with sub-standard presentations and preparation.

'Well. Get on with it.'

He moved around from the back of the auditorium where he had seated himself, walked down the stairs and then stood before us all. He was already irritating me. Knowing, as he did, that he was to present today, it made no sense for him to have seated himself at the back of the auditorium. He should have been sitting at the front, ready to start. No forethought.

'The case I would like to discuss today is a 65-year-old man I saw yesterday who presented to the casualty department with blood in his pee . . .'

'Stop!' I stood up. He must have learned his medicine from the *Women's Weekly*. 'If you are going to be a doctor, then please talk like a doctor. What is pee? What is blood in the pee? You are not giving this talk to the local rotary club. This is your chance to impress me, and you will not impress me talking like a primary-school student.' I had to convert these lay people to doctors.

'Sorry. I'll start again.' Exasperated tones from the Professor of Surgery – he knew this was not a good start.

'Good idea,' I advised, the sarcasm dripping from my mouth.

'I would like to discuss the case of a 65-year-old who presented to casualty yesterday with a three-day history of hematuria.' He was cautious and was now talking to me rather than to the audience.

'Good. Much better. Stop there.' I stood up and looked at the audience. 'OK. What are you thinking? You. What do you think?' I pointed to an anorexic-looking woman wearing a black jumper over black jeans with long black strands of hair that essentially covered her face. I hated the Goth look.

'He could have a tumour?' she said tentatively, unsure of herself and her possible diagnosis.

'I could have a tumour. What are you trying to tell me?' She was not going to get away with rubbish.

'He could have kidney tumour . . . a cancer?' She spoke almost in whispers.

'He could have anything! He could have a house on the beach. What is YOUR tentative diagnosis? Give me three possibilities.' She was now red in the face. Embarrassed. Silent. She could not string the words together.

'Anyone else?' I looked around the class.

Hands went up. 'You in the front. What is your name?' This one was one of only three students wearing a tie and a white coat. Impressive.

'He could have bladder cancer, a renal stone, or he could have had some renal trauma.'

This one was good. 'Well done. So what else do you want to know? What questions would you ask?'

The banter went on for an hour or so, with questions and answers until the case had been thoroughly described. The possibilities had been analysed and the pathology dissected. Socrates had a lot to answer for.

My old Professor of Surgery used to talk about 'thalamic learning'. The thalamus was the part of the brain that governed and controlled emotion.

'For a student to learn,' he would say, 'their thalamus needs to be engaged. They need to feel the fright of not knowing.'

I used to hate him for his humiliating style. However, there is no question that I have never forgotten the lessons I learned with him. I tried to use a blend of compassion but with a certain toughness, which made a student appreciate there are dire consequences to not knowing.

'How would you treat this patient?' was an old nugget that always frightened them. The slightest hesitation and you painted reality for them.

'In less than six months' time you might have a patient very similar to this. You will be alone at 3 am, having to make a decision. Do you call the consultant? Do you just go ahead and do it yourself? What are you going to do? How are you to sort it out? This is why we have these tutorials, so that students can simulate various scenarios in a safe environment, in an environment where all that will be lost is a varying amount of pride rather than a patient's life.'

There was always silence. Silence of men and women realising that the safety of school and the ephemeral safety of the term 'student' were soon to be taken away from them. I imagined they had the same feelings and look the day their parents made them stop sucking their thumbs or took away their favourite blanket – frightened rabbits in headlights.

'The right thing to do when you are ever unsure – and I guarantee you will all be unsure – is to call for senior help. Always remember that. We have all been there. We have all had the same uncertainty, the same fears and emotions. Some of us will be awful when you ring us. Get your story straight and make it short. You ring me at three in the morning and start stuttering out some difficult-to-understand sob story about a patient and I will fall asleep or get angry. Get it straight and to the point. OK. Now who has a poem for us today?'

The students had been very uncomfortable about reading poetry in a surgical tutorial when they first started with me. I insisted that each week one of them would bring in a poem to share with the rest of us.

'Poets spend their entire lives studying humanity, the same humanity, suffering and anguish you are about to spend your lives ministering to. You know about the science of surgery, you will soon find out about the business of surgery . . . but this is your chance to learn about the art of surgery. If you cannot acknowledge the humanity of your patients, then you will not be good doctors. You will be technicians. Mechanics.'

It took some convincing at first, but now they looked forward to these sessions. They enjoyed the repose during their otherwise hectic and lost week.

A young girl came forward. 'I have a poem entitled 'Human Seasons', and it's by John Keats.' She was timid.

'Why did you choose this poem?' I asked her.

'Well, it reminds me that we are all, our patients and us, are on the same journey through life. We are not immune to what they go through. We too will become old one day.'

'Fine. That is lovely, please read it to us.'

She started and was immediately transformed into another place. There was intense silence in the room:

Four seasons fill the measure of the year;
There are four seasons in the mind of Man:
He has his lusty Spring, when fancy clear
Takes in all beauty with an easy span:
He has his Summer, when luxuriously
Spring's honeyed cud of youthful thought he loves
To ruminate, and by such dreaming high

Is nearest unto heaven: quiet coves
His soul has in its Autumn, when his wings
He furleth close; contented so to look
On mists in idleness – to let fair things
Pass by unheeded as a threshold brook: –
He has his Winter too of pale misfeature,
Or else he would forgo his mortal nature.

We discussed the poem as we always did, students drawing
analogies to patients they had treated and seen during their
short careers. I still had a few minutes before I was due in
my rooms to see one of my last sessions of patients, but it
was time to wind up my final class.

'You know, ladies and gentlemen, this is my last day in
surgery. I will not be here next week.' There were gasps of
disbelief around the room. There were some who wanted
to say, 'Please do not do it; do not go.' Most, however, were
intrigued at the bravery of one, as senior as I was, taking the
road less travelled. Doing something that was totally different and leaving in his prime.

'Surgery has been good to me.' I felt I needed to say
something to this new generation. Leave them with some
words of advice to guide their path.

'You are extraordinary human beings on the brink of the
greatest of all careers that any could ever hope to have. You
have, within your grasp, the ability to alleviate suffering,
to take away pain, to cure disease and, most importantly, to
know when to let nature take its course. Above all, stay true
to yourselves.

'This is not a business. This is a calling, and the day you
stop thinking of it as a calling is the day you must leave.
You are more than technicians; you are society's confidant,

conscience and high priest all rolled into one. When you study your books, you are studying the wisdom of those whose life was spent finding more knowledge. You use this knowledge to effect good. What you do is incredibly brave. Few in society have the courage to take the decisions that you will need to take daily. It is OK to be scared. But do not be paralysed by it. When you are scared, hand the reigns to others. Ask for help. There is nothing worse than the doctor who puts ego ahead of a patient's welfare.

'There is so much I want to tell you. Above all, help your patients to understand the consequences of what you do and the consequences of doing nothing. You need to advise them as if they are your own. Treat them with respect, and love them. They are you and you are them.'

I stopped talking. I had just given a lecture that reminded me of Polonius advising Laertes prior to his departure, in Shakespeare's *Hamlet*. There was so much left unexpressed. How do I help these doctors to be human? 'Please continue to read poetry. Listen to music. I know some of you play instruments – just keep doing it. Balance knife with wife and with life. That is the answer. Balance . . .' I was raving now.

I turned and left. Behind me, I heard applause.

I refused valedictions. I refused to return congratulatory notes. I simply left.

*

It is only now, some years later, that I am able to pen my thoughts about surgery once again. It is only now that I can relive my years – the internships, the resident years, to registrar and then private practice. In my academic practice, my research, have I done any good as a surgeon?

I progressed from self-obsession, to arrogance, to immense humility and then to the paralysis of fear. Fear of the unknown land awaiting us all. There are those who will remember me well and those for whom the evil that I have inadvertently done should, as it did for Julius Caesar, live after me, while the good is interred with my bones.

All surgeons make mistakes. How many operations had I done that I should not have done? That I should have known would not alleviate a patient's suffering but rather condemn them to a life of anguish. How many lives could I have saved with more skill, more knowledge? How many interns, residents and registrars had I influenced negatively instead of inspiring? Who knows. What is done is done.

I had never done any of these knowingly, of course. But the retrospectoscope is a cruel instrument, and when shone on one's career past it is crueller still.

Perhaps one day I will return, after my sojourn in education and business. Perhaps there is one set of rooms still in me, one final operating list undone, one final cut to be made. One patient whose life will teach me the meaning of my own.

Till then, I float with an emptiness where surgery used to be. At night, when all is still, I am left once again with the thoughts and memories of what has been a surgical life.

At 47, Jonathan Brewster finally feels like he's king of the world – he has a lucrative job, a happy marriage, two children in private schools, an impressive house and a flashy car. He's also hugely in debt, but that's never really bothered him – until he wakes up at dawn bursting for the toilet, urinates blood and ends up waiting eight hours in Emergency before he sees a doctor. In the midst of his successful life, Jonathan has neglected to take care of his health, or even to conceive of the possibility of losing it.

Urologist Mohamed Khadra comes into contact with this patient as he enters a maze of diagnosis and treatment for what turns out to be bladder cancer. For Dr Khadra, Jonathan goes from being just another patient to something much more, as his own battle with cancer puts them on the same side of the doctor–patient relationship.

From the author of the bestselling *Making the Cut* comes this gripping non-fiction story of a stranger in the strangest of lands: the Australian health-care system. It is both a manual for patients, families and health-care workers and a moving examination of the human spirit.

AVAILABLE NOW IN ALL GOOD BOOKSHOPS